How to Pass the UK Fire Service Interview

A Step-by-Step Insider's Guide

READING SOMEONE ELSE'S BOOK?

SCAN THE QR CODE TO GET YOUR OWN!

Contents

Foreword

There is an enormous amount of competition for every vacancy in the Fire and Rescue Service. Every year tens of thousands of people apply to join.

More than 1,000 candidates applied for just six firefighter positions in Shropshire Fire and Rescue Service recently – that's 167 applicants per job. This is pretty much the standard ratio for a UK fire service recruitment process. It's very rare to get fewer than 100 applicants per vacancy.

It's a sought-after job, so you really need to stand out if you are going to get in. You need to perform better than 100+ other people in the interview. You quite literally need to be in the top 1% to pass.

Only those who perform *exceptionally well* in the recruitment process are successful in landing their dream job, and to be able to perform exceptionally well, you have to *prepare* exceptionally well. The fire service has very specific requirements though, so when we talk about preparing *well* we don't just mean preparing *hard*, we mean preparing in exactly the right way.

It does require hard work, but also planning and direction, without which your hard work is a waste of time. This book does most of the planning and gives you all the direction you need to make sure your efforts pay off. You'll still need to put in some work to get yourself ready though, or you'll probably lose out to someone else who did. The Army summed it up nicely...

"Proper preparation and planning prevents poor performance."

This book takes that phrase literally and guides you through every step of how to properly prepare and plan to pass the Fire Service interview.

You Already Ha  !

Congratulations – you made a very wise decision by choosing this book to assist you in passing your Fire Service interview. You now have a huge advantage over anyone who is preparing blind.

There are currently several books available claiming to offer help and advice on how to pass the Firefighter Selection Process. A few of them offer one or two useful tips but most are either outdated or written for an American audience. Some are merely unhelpful, but many are, unfortunately, very misleading. If you have read any other books purporting to help you with your interview, **please forget everything you have read. This is the only book you need.** This may sound like a big-headed statement, but it's backed-up by hundreds of emails from grateful and successful readers.

This book is the only one available which is focused entirely on how to pass the UK interview process, written by a serving middle manager, currently working in the recruitment process within a UK Fire and Rescue Service.

This book wastes no time dealing with the medical and physical stages; that information is readily available for free online.

You are going to learn some simple yet effective techniques to prepare for your interview and some key methods to help you excel on the big day itself.

It's a sad fact that **having all the right skills and personal qualities and great experience is not enough to get you through the Fire and Rescue Service interview**; you need to tailor your responses in certain specific ways to show your interviewer that you've done your homework, and you know what is required in the modern Fire and Rescue Service.

Using the information in this manual, you can show your interviewer that you not only have the right experience but that you have the right mind-set and that you will fit in as a valuable member of the team.

This book will ensure you can present your skills, experience and aptitude in a way that cries out *"Fire Service Material"* to your interviewer.

About the Author

Andy Smith has been heavily involved in UK Fire Service interview processes since 2005 across two separate Fire and Rescue Services and has worked collaboratively with several others. He is currently the lead-officer responsible for the recruitment process in a major UK Fire and Rescue Service, writing the interview questions, training the interviewers, conducting the interviews themselves, assessing performance and providing feedback, both for interviewers and interviewees. He has interviewed countless hopefuls trying to get into the Fire and Rescue Service, hoping to become both Retained (On-Call) and Wholetime Firefighters as well as interviewing existing personnel trying to gain promotion to Crew, Watch and Station Manager.

Through the National Fire Chief's Council (**NFCC**) and several working groups, the author is able to keep abreast of current interview trends and themes in Fire and Rescue Services from England, Scotland, Wales, and Northern Ireland. He has successfully guided countless individuals from all regions through the recruitment process. Within the Fire Service, the author has held roles within the training and development arenas and has developed a keen understanding of the most effective methods of coaching and mentoring – essential skills in anyone passing on knowledge and advice.

There can be few people currently writing in the UK with a better insight into what it takes to succeed in a Fire and Rescue Service interview.

In this book he combines his gift for teaching with his inside knowledge of Fire Service recruitment to produce a winning formula. He has developed a unique method that takes a candidate's existing life experiences and develops them into impressive, polished, and well-rounded answers tailored to any Fire Service interview question. It is as close to a "recipe for success" as you're ever likely to get.

Preface

I have seen a lot of very good people fail the Fire and Rescue Service interview. People who have what it takes to be a great Firefighter regularly blow their chances by performing poorly in the interview room.

It is a particular problem with ex-military candidates. Every year I interview people who have just left the armed forces and would no doubt thrive in the Fire Service if they could just get over the interview hurdle. The examples they give in the interview start off sounding great, but just aren't presented in the correct "Fire Service" way. People seem to think an *impressive sounding* story is enough, but it isn't. I have heard some stories of truly heroic deeds and impressive feats from some obviously very capable people, but they still failed the interview because of the way they delivered their responses. A Fire Service interview tests you on *very specific criteria* and if you don't know these criteria, you stand a very slim chance of succeeding.

The system is flawed because the best candidates often get rejected. I do what I can to change things from within by setting more relevant questions, but I still feel sympathy for the good people who fail because they didn't know the system. Whenever we reject someone like this, I wish I could get hold of them and help them. This book is my attempt to do that.

Hopefully you're just beginning your journey into the Fire Service, so you can start using this book from the outset, in good time before your interview. If your interview is tomorrow, well you've left it too late to do the full-prep. In that case, use your few available hours familiarising yourself with the PQAs or the NFCC Leadership Framework in Parts 3 and 4.

If you've already failed one or more interviews, do not worry. Failure is more common than success due to the intense competition. Next time, with this guidance, you'll be better prepared than every previous time and far better prepared than 99% of the other candidates. This book has helped hundreds of people succeed since the first edition was published back in 2018, and thanks to its annual updates it's still the best prep available. Think positively.

To complete this book properly, you need to set aside an hour or two a week to make sure you are fully prepared when the big day comes. You're going to be doing some writing, thinking, rehearsal and possibly some actual work if you are lacking experience in any areas. Think about the best time for you, when you can work without disturbances or distractions. Ideally a set day or a set point in your shift pattern, so it becomes part of your routine. You need to commit a couple of hours a week, but the end result will be worth it. Depending on your circumstances, the best time for you may be when your kids have gone to bed and you've had your dinner, when your partner is in the gym, whenever, just as long as you can concentrate. You need an A4 notebook too, to be used *only* for Fire Service interview prep, nothing else.

Read this book in order, completing each task fully before moving on to the next part. If you try dipping in and out randomly you will probably get confused and you definitely won't get the full benefit. Any terms or acronyms you don't recognise – check the glossary at the back.

Together we will get you fully prepped for the interview. It's going to take a fair bit of work, but it will be worth it in the end. The harder you work now, the easier it will be to excel in your interview. Think *"Train hard, fight easy"*.

One last thing, if you find this book helpful, *please* give it a positive review on Amazon (even if you got it somewhere else). I get lots of emails saying, *"Loving the book but not reviewing it as I don't want anyone else to know about it until I pass the interview!"* If that's you, please don't forget to come back and review – tell others how the book helped you achieve your goal. This way we can get more of the right people into the job.

If you have any criticisms, comments or suggestions, please email me – the book is updated every year and information from readers helps to make sure it's always totally current and relevant.

My email address is getinto999@gmail.com
Good luck! Andy Smith, 2025

STOP!

You Need Something Else First!

You're not just going to be a passive reader here.

You need to get yourself an A4-size (preferably hardback), lined notebook.

You will be making a lot of notes!

Over the course of this book, you will be filling in key information in the notebook until eventually, your notebook will have become your bible, containing all the information you need to get through the interview. Don't use your notebook book for anything else. It's not a rough pad for writing shopping lists or a sketch book for your kid. It's your best chance of getting the job you really want. Take it seriously!

Part 1 – Your Motivation

Why do you want to get into the Fire and Rescue Service (**FRS**)? You need to have a think about your motivations as you may be asked about them. For me, it was a couple of things. Firstly, I was stuck in a boring, dead-end job with no promotion prospects and an ever-present threat of redundancy. I'd been doing it for years and I hated it. I wanted something more interesting, more varied, more secure, and maybe more exciting. I wasn't getting any younger and realised I needed to make a change soon. Also, I wanted to do a respectable job; one I could be proud of. I hated the way people yawned whenever I tried to explain my tedious job to them, and I could tell they wish they'd never asked. I envied people who could just say a one-word job title and be instantly understood; instantly respected: "Pilot... Surgeon... Soldier... Teacher... Paramedic...*Firefighter*." But it wasn't a vanity thing; I didn't crave admiration, it was about self-respect and self-esteem, *confidence*. I wanted to be able to be proud of what I did. I wanted to know that my kids and my partner are proud of me too.

Perhaps most importantly though, I felt that I might have the potential to do something better; I felt that I was wasted behind a desk. I felt like I could help people in some way if I just had the chance, rather than working in an office to make money for someone else. I might be able to make a difference to the world, even if it was only a small contribution in my local area. The more I learned about the role of Firefighter, the more I realised it was the ideal role for me. I could see that it offered the chance to improve myself by learning new skills and to work as part of a big team. I could see that the Fire and Rescue Service looks after its employees and gives them the chance to thrive. I could see that I would be given the opportunity to do a *good job*, in every sense, and that the harder I tried, the better I would become, and the more difference I would make to the wider community. The Fire Service was my chance to be the best I could be. It was also my chance to drive around with blue lights and sirens and get paid for using the gym!

Without realising it, I had hit upon a winning combination. I had linked my own ambitions and urge to improve myself with my desire to help others.

Whenever I thought about how I wanted to learn new skills and progress within the Fire Service, I realised that doing so would improve my ability to help others – a more highly skilled, well-rounded, and competent Firefighter is better able to help their community. No matter how selfish my motivation was to improve myself, I would always be able to justify my desire to succeed by linking it to my ability to serve the people of my area.

TASK 1

Get your fresh, new A4 notebook out. At the top of a page, write "MOTIVATIONS". Then list as many reasons as you can why you want to join the Fire Service. This shouldn't take longer than five minutes but will come in useful later. Envisage yourself as a Firefighter and think what aspects of your life will be better in that role. The more honest you are, the more useful this list will be later on. Examples may include Personal *pride, job security, fitness, pension, image, helping others, challenges, new skills, cool uniform, saving lives, excitement, self-esteem, desirability, want to follow in someone's footsteps, bored in current job, teamwork* etc.

They don't all have to be *good* reasons, just *real* reasons. Give each reason a number; if your main reason is that you want to save lives, give that a "10". If, say, getting your LGV licence is a fairly minor factor, give that a "4", for example.

We'll link back to these reasons later when writing your interview answers.

PART 1 – SUMMARY

Well done, you have made a start on preparing for your dream job. By reflecting on your motivation, you have taken very important first step. Part One was nice and straightforward. So easy, in fact, you might want to make a start on Part Two whilst you're at it!

Part 2 – Your Understanding of the Fire and Rescue Service

It's not About Being a Hero

So, you're pretty keen to get into the Fire and Rescue Service, right? The fact that you're reading this suggests you are. If you're keen, then you've probably thought long and hard about what it would be like to be a Firefighter. Maybe you know some Firefighters already; perhaps you're part of a Fire Service group on social media or maybe you're a Retained/On-Call Firefighter struggling to pass the Wholetime interview. Maybe you have family in the Fire and Rescue Service. Maybe none of the above. Whatever is true in your case, it is likely that you will have a reasonably realistic idea of what life is like as a Firefighter and you know not to expect to be performing daily acts of heroism and bravery. Many Fire Services now make candidates complete a questionnaire before applying to ensure they understand that they will be spending much more time performing Community Safety activities than rescuing babies from burning buildings.

Just in case you don't already realise it though, let me spell this out. *This job is not about being a hero*. No interviewer working for any Fire and Rescue Service in the United Kingdom is currently looking to recruit the bravest, most heroic candidate. That kind of person isn't necessarily suited to the modern Fire Service. The job now involves a huge range of different kinds of work, such as visiting people at home to conduct safety and wellbeing checks and talking to schoolchildren about hoax calls/playing with matches; it's more important that you're a decent, enthusiastic, approachable and considerate person than a hero. I can guarantee that you will spend a thousandth of the time rescuing people from burning buildings as you will spend fitting smoke alarms in elderly people's houses. It is vitally important that you understand this when going into an interview.

KEY POINT

If you were hoping to impress the interviewer about the time you risked your life jumping off a bridge to save someone from drowning, or the time you ran into a burning building to drag someone out... forget it. No fire service wants reckless risk-takers.

One interviewer I know from another Fire Service used to ask applicants the following icebreaker question: *"How accurate do you think* Backdraft *or* Station 19 *are at representing life as a Firefighter?"* He said the best answer he received was from a young cockney who replied *"About as accurate as* EastEnders *is at representing life in London, in other words, not very. They exaggerate the exciting bits and leave out all the mundane day-to-day stuff."* He went on to talk about community safety, training, testing and maintenance of equipment, admin, and cleaning, thus showing that he had a very realistic and grounded understanding of what life in the Fire Service is all about. As it was just an "icebreaker" question, the answer wasn't marked, but the interviewer immediately found himself warming to the candidate, which may have influenced his scoring. The candidate was successful.

The firefighters who entered Grenfell Tower time after time in such challenging conditions – some whilst fearing for their own lives – acted with great courage, and similar smaller-scale acts of bravery happen regularly in Fire Services throughout the UK. I am certainly not belittling actual acts of heroism and bravery or claiming that bravery isn't an important quality in the modern Firefighter. The point is that no UK Fire Service is currently *assessing a candidate's bravery* at the interview stage of the selection process.

So now you've abandoned all thoughts of demonstrating your heroism in the interview, you need to get a full understanding of what your chosen Fire Service is all about. First though, you need to know some details about the UK Fire and Rescue Service in general.

Basic Knowledge of Laws Relating the Fire and Rescue Service

There are over fifty Fire Services in the UK and whilst they all have their differences, there are certain things which apply to all of them – the laws which control and guide them. As with any workplace, certain generic laws apply, such as the Disability Discrimination Act, Equality Act, Health and Safety at Work Act etc., but here we are going to focus on the specific ones which directly govern the Fire Service.

The main one in England and Wales is the *Fire and Rescue Services Act 2004*. North of the border, the *Fire (Scotland) Act 2005* applies, and it's equally obvious where the *Fire and Rescue Services (Northern Ireland) Order 2006* applies.

You don't need to get too bogged-down with these.

Just know the name of the one that covers the area you're applying for and remember that it is the piece of law that governs the duties and powers of the Fire Service.

Basically, these laws mean that every Fire Service has to:

1. Promote fire safety.
2. Fight fires.
3. Protect people and property from fires.
4. Rescue people from road traffic incidents.
5. Deal with other specific emergencies, such as flooding or terrorist attack; and
6. Do other things to respond to the needs of their communities and the risks they face.

There are an ever increasing (post-Grenfell) number of other laws which relate to your chosen Fire and Rescue Service, relating to Fire Safety and also one relating to Emergency Planning. We will look into these in detail in Task 2.

You can see the main three laws relate to your Fire and Rescue Service in the following table:

Region	Legislation		
	Primary Legislation	Fire Safety Legislation	Emergency Planning
England & Wales	Fire and Rescue Services Act 2004	Regulatory Reform (Fire Safety) Order 2005	Civil Contingencies Act 2004
Scotland	Fire (Scotland) Act 2005	Fire Safety (Scotland) Regulations 2006	Civil Contingencies Act 2004
Northern Ireland	Fire and Rescue Service (N.I.) Order 2006	Fire Safety Regulations (Northern Ireland) 2010	

This table shows which legislation relates to your chosen Fire Service – use it for Task 2.

If you find this kind of thing interesting and want to know more, here are some links where you can obtain further information. Don't worry if you are not too interested in this bit – very few Firefighters are!

Fire and Rescue Services Act.................................... www.is.gd/frsa2004
Regulatory Reform (Fire Safety) Order................... www.is.gd/rro2005
Civil Contingencies Act... www.is.gd/cca2004
Fire (Scotland) Act... www.is.gd/fsa2005
Fire and Rescue (N.I.) Order..................................... www.is.gd/frsni2006

TASK 2

(This is good background stuff but don't spend more than an hour on it.)

At the top of a new page in your notebook, write the heading "**LEGISLATION**". Under this heading, write the names of the three laws that govern your Fire Service, using the above table. Write down a summary of each one (we've summed up the main one already with the above list of six responsibilities).

Perfectly good summaries of each of these acts can be found on Wikipedia. Basically, the Fire Safety legislation is all about keeping people safe from the risks of fire in shops, offices, hospitals, hotels, communal areas of blocks of flats etc. It is the law that prosecutes landlords for locking fire exits, checks on overcrowding, requires proper emergency lighting, signage, alarms, fire doors etc. It was in the news a lot after Grenfell and applies to pretty much every building apart from private houses. Lots of extra pieces of legislation such as the Building Safety Act 2022; Fire Safety Act 2021 and the Fire Safety (England) Regulations 2022 have been introduced, mainly to improve safety in blocks of flats and address issues relating to cladding and breaches in compartmentation.

The *Civil Contingencies Act* is all about different organisations (emergency services, local authorities, environment agencies, utilities companies etc.) working together to plan for emergencies (pandemics, terrorist attacks etc.). It directs these organisations to conduct exercises, share information with each other, and communicate with the public.

After this task you should have a page summarising the three main Acts relating to your Fire and Rescue Service and very brief summaries of the new fire safety laws. As a Firefighter you won't be expected to be an expert in any of them, but interviewers have asked which laws apply to the Fire Service; the above information is enough for a Firefighter interview.

Also, be aware of who governs your chosen Fire Service; whether it's Westminster, Welsh Assembly, Scottish or Northern Irish Government and the name of the person in charge – the Chief Fire Officer or Commissioner.

It's also worth noting that as a result of the Grenfell Tower fire another piece of legislation, the Fire Safety (England) Regulations 2022 has been introduced to force those responsible for fire safety in high-rise blocks of flats to implement additional safety measures and provide information to Fire and Rescue Services to help them plan and provide an effective operational response.

Also, in response to the Grenfell, The Regulatory Reform (Fire Safety) Order has been changed by the Fire Safety Act 2021 to cover external cladding, balconies, flat doors, windows and building structure in a way that it didn't previously; and by part of the Building Safety Act 2022 to place new responsibilities on landlords like giving safety information to residents.

That's enough of the legislation stuff, and almost certainly more than you'll need for an interview. It's possible that you won't have to use any of it at all in the interview, but we've covered it here, so you don't get caught out.

What the Modern Fire and Rescue Service Actually Does.

It's infuriating how many candidates give terrible answers to questions about the work we do in the Fire Service. The usual question is something like *"Apart from fires and RTCs* [**Road Traffic Collisions**]*, what kind of work do you think Westhamptonshire Fire and Rescue Service is involved with?"*

As soon as candidates realise that they can't talk about the most obvious things – fires and car crashes – they tend to get flustered and sometimes actually give up, looking embarrassed! A great job opportunity thrown away by lack of preparation. Luckily for you, I've done all the hard work for you.

First though, a quick little exercise.

TASK 3

On a new page in your notebook, write the heading **"THE ROLE OF THE MODERN FIRE AND RESCUE SERVICE"**.

Divide the page in two down the middle – on the left side write **"REACTIVE"** and on the right side right **"PREVENTATIVE"**. Now list as many of each as you can.

Reactive (or "Response") work is when the Fire Service responds to a call, so fires and RTCs would be reactive. **Preventative** work is anything aimed at reducing the risk of people coming to harm in the first place, like fitting smoke alarms or conducting school talks.

Give yourself a couple of minutes and see how many you can think of, including the examples I've just given you. Compare your examples with the ones on the next page and copy any you missed into your notebook.

You won't have time to talk about all of these activities. **Highlight 5 or 6 from each category that you feel most comfortable talking about**. These are the ones you need to remember for the interview.

Don't be disheartened if you couldn't think of many. Some of them are not obvious and if you don't know anyone in the Fire Service then it's no surprise that you didn't know about them.

All Fire Services are involved in multiple projects and initiatives, but here are some examples of the things many of the UK's Fire Services are currently, or have recently been involved with:

Reactive work includes animal rescues (not just cats from trees but also farm/domestic/wild animals from ditches and ravines, pets like cats and snakes from ducts and cavity walls etc.); rescues from height (people stuck on cliffs or tall structures, often suicidal, drunk or on drugs); confined space rescues (sewers, silos etc.); bariatric (obese) rescues (often by removing/reinforcing parts of homes, making ramps to first floor windows, removing roofs and using cranes to get a patient out); assisting the ambulance service; trauma care; responding to cardiac arrests (Fire Medical Response or FMR); flooding (pumping out properties etc.); inland water rescues (saving people from rivers, lakes and reservoirs but not sea); transport incidents (rail and tram crashes, ship fires, plane crashes); lift rescues; rescues from collapsed structures; HazMat (hazardous materials) incidents; chemical spills (identification, containment and clear up or wash-down); responding to carbon monoxide alarms; CBRNe (chemical, biological, radiological, nuclear and explosives) incidents; decontamination of the public; ring removal; helping people who are locked in or out; fire investigation; rescuing people who are trapped in machinery (usually on farms or in factories); and MTA (Marauding Terrorist Attack) response.

This list is not exhaustive, and your chosen FRS may not be involved in all of these activities; they may be involved in additional ones not mentioned.

Preventative work includes youth engagement activities (school talks on hoax calling or arson, working with probation or youth workers to educate young fire-setters); retrieval of abandoned gas cylinders; arson prevention (working with other agencies to identify possible targets and make them safer); grassfire prevention; work around Halloween and bonfire night (youth education, collaboration with the police and working with Trading Standards to check the sale of fireworks); employability schemes (helping 2nd or 3rd generation unemployed get into work); Young Firefighters schemes; Fire Safety inspections of businesses / care homes / hospitals / takeaways / blocks of flats / schools etc.; road safety campaigns (drink / drug driving, mobile phone / seatbelt awareness, motorcycle safety, post-speeding driver awareness course input); open days; home safety / safe-and-well visits (checking cooking and smoking habits, escape routes, electrics and fitting smoke alarms); fly-tipping prevention; delivering talks to community / faith / elderly / vulnerable groups; and working with partner agencies to plan for major events/incidents.

As you can see, there's a lot more to the Fire and Rescue Service than just "Fire" and "Rescue" – you've probably filled most of a page with that! As the number of fire calls is declining, the modern Fire Service is diversifying into many different areas, all aimed at improving the safety and wellbeing of the communities it serves.

Some Fire Services are now visiting people at home and assessing their level of health and fitness and offering smoking cessation advice as well as providing guidance on diet and exercise. Whereas they used to just fit smoke alarms, many Firefighters are now expected to assess people's wellbeing and look out for slip, trip and fall hazards as well as being alert to signs of isolation, hoarding, loneliness, dementia, cuckooing (using a vulnerable person's house for drug-dealing), domestic/child abuse, modern slavery and radicalisation.

All this has to be done with dwindling resources, so collaboration with other agencies is vital. You can't get away with just squirting a hose anymore!

KEY POINT

The Fire and Rescue Service is now involved in a vast range of activities besides firefighting and responding to RTCs. These activities are all aimed at improving the safety and wellbeing of the community and often have to be done with diminishing resources, meaning cooperation with other agencies is essential.

It is often said that the Fire and Rescue Service is a victim of its own success; its preventative home safety work has contributed to a 33% decrease in fires since the early 2010's, but this doesn't mean Firefighters are less busy. There has been a simultaneous increase in other types of incidents of nearly 50%. These include RTCs, flooding, medical incidents and effecting entry or exit.

Equality, Diversity and Inclusion.

This is a key subject you <u>must</u> understand before your interview.

First, a couple of statistics to get you thinking:

- Approximately **41%** of *people* in the UK are white males
- Approximately **95%** of *firefighters* in the UK are white males

In years gone by when firefighters mainly just extinguished fires and then left, this inequality may not have mattered as much (apart from the obvious lack of job opportunities for minority groups) as a fire doesn't care about the race or gender of the person pumping water onto it. Operationally, a completely white, male fire service may have been perfectly effective in its role. The 21st century Firefighter though, as we have seen, is increasingly involved in risk-reduction and community work, so it is becoming more important that the Fire Service reflects the communities it serves, in order to understand and engage more effectively with people.

Fire and Rescue Services across the UK are under pressure to encourage more women and people from black, Asian and minority ethnic (**BAME**) backgrounds to apply for jobs. This does not mean that the selection process is being made easier for people based on their background (which would be *'positive discrimination'*, and illegal); it just means Fire Services are trying to get more women and people from BAME backgrounds to *apply* in the first place (which is *'positive action'*, and legal). As well as being beneficial in improving community relations and ensuring equality of opportunity, it's a no-brainer for an employer – would you rather recruit from a pool consisting only of white men, or a far bigger pool of *the entire population*?

The government has been demanding Fire and Rescue Services address Equality, Diversity and Inclusion (**E,D&I,** or sometimes just **E&D**) issues for years, and yet as recently as January 2024 an independent review into the culture of one Fire Service found problems relating to misogyny and bullying. A separate report by His Majesty's Inspectorate of Constabulary and Fire & Rescue Services (HMICFRS) in 2023 found evidence of racism, sexism, and homophobia in at least 11 fire and rescue services and in November 2022;

and an independent report into London Fire Brigade by former chief prosecutor Nazir Afzal labelled the brigade *"institutionally misogynist and racist"*. This is a likely interview topic, as many fire services are currently awaiting reports into their own cultures, with unpleasant results expected.

Even if there is no specific E,D&I question in the interview, it is possible you are being marked on your E,D&I awareness whilst answering the other questions. There are some simple things you can do to ensure you are both prepared for an E,D&I question and able to answer all the other questions in a way which shows you are aware of E,D&I issues.

Firstly, let's make sure you know what Equality, Diversity & Inclusion means:

Equality is defined in law (The Equality Act 2010) and is about ensuring people are not treated differently or less favourably because of any one of...

Nine Protected Characteristics:

1. **Race**
2. **Gender**
3. **Disability**
4. **Religion/belief**
5. **Sexual orientation**
6. **Gender reassignment**
7. **Marriage/civil partnership**
8. **Pregnancy/maternity**
9. **Age.**

Note: Equity is often used instead of Equality. Equity is when resources and opportunities are provided based on individual needs to achieve an equal outcome, whereas Equality tends to focus on treating everyone the same, regardless of their needs or circumstances. For example, making sure everyone has access to free smoke alarms regardless of their characteristics is *equality*; whereas making sure people with hearing difficulties are provided with flashing strobe smoke alarms is *equity*.

Diversity is about promoting everybody's right to be different, free from discrimination, valued as an individual; to have choice and dignity with a right to your own beliefs and values. Diversity is about creating a culture which values individual differences and encourages people to be themselves at work.

Inclusion is about creating an environment where all individuals feel valued, respected, and supported. It involves actively inviting participation from diverse groups and ensuring everyone has a sense of belonging and the opportunity to thrive.

A good guide to all things Equality can be found on the Equalities and Human Rights Commission website, here: **www.equalityhumanrights.com**

Secondly, find out what your chosen Fire Service is doing to further the E,D&I agenda in their area. They may have an Equality/Equity Statement or Policy available on their website detailing how they intend to meet their obligations. **If they state what percentage of their workforce comes from different backgrounds, this information is gold; you need to record it in your book.**

Thirdly, find out the key stats about the area served by your chosen Fire Service, such as percentage of people identifying themselves as BAME. There may not be stats available for all of the different Protected Characteristics in your particular region; in these cases, UK stats will do. For instance, according to the 2021 census, 18% of the UK population is BAME and 51% of the UK population is female – compare that with the percentage of BAME and female firefighters in your chosen Fire Service and you're likely to find quite a discrepancy.

Lastly, check your vocabulary, so you don't use outdated words, especially *Fireman* (always use *Firefighter*). In fact, avoid any terms which use the word *man,* such as *policeman, manpower, man-hours, chairman, layman* etc. Instead use non-gender-specific terms like *police officer, personnel, working hours, chair, layperson* etc. Don't use *he* or *him* when referring to generic human beings, just use *they* or *them.* Don't take it too far though – obviously use masculine words if you're talking about a specific man.

The term *minority ethnic* acknowledges the fact that we all belong to ethnic groups and is now preferable to *ethnic minority.* Avoid the generic and obsolete *coloured* at all costs. Avoid *The Handicapped* or *The Disabled.* Instead use *people with disabilities,* putting the person first.

Avoid passive, victim words. Use language that respects people with disabilities as active individuals with control over their own lives. *Cripple, and invalid* are totally obsolete and absolutely unacceptable. If these words do not already seem highly offensive to you, then you definitely need to focus on your E,D&I awareness.

Regarding this last point, try not to tie yourself up in knots worrying about which "politically correct" phrase you should be using. Your interviewer is not expecting you to be the perfect finished article and will forgive you for using some of the less offensive outdated words like *manpower* especially if, for instance, you're fresh out of the armed forces having had no diversity training. Just try and make sure that you use the correct terminology when writing your answers out later, so you rehearse using the right terms.

TASK 4

On a new page, write the heading "**EQUALITY, DIVERSITY & INCLUSION**".

- Write down the definitions of Equality, Equity, Diversity & Inclusion in your own words, in a way that you'll remember.
- Summarise your chosen Fire Service's website's statements on Equality, Equity, Diversity & Inclusion – the policy and actions they are taking.
- Research your chosen Fire Service's area and write down key stats about the population's characteristics. Note any discrepancies between your Fire Service and the population it serves.

For example: *"3% of Westhampton FRS staff are BAME compared with 22% in the local population. 13% of WFRS staff are female compared with 51% of the UK."*

Don't panic. You are not going to have to do masses of research or remember pages of stats here; this exercise is just designed to get you thinking about E,D&I in your area. Hopefully a couple of memorable things will crop up. You will refer back to the work you have done here when preparing your answers later.

Whilst doing this research you may come across some alarming reports about cultural problems in your chosen service (more on this in the next section).

KEY POINTS

Most fire services place a *huge* emphasis on Equality/Equity, Diversity & Inclusion (E,D&I or sometimes just Equality & Diversity, E&D).

Fire and Rescue Services across the UK are under pressure to make sure the diversity of their staff reflects the communities they serve.

Many Fire and Rescue Servies are currently undergoing independent reviews which are likely to result in some pretty unpleasant reading (London Fire Brigade was found to be *"institutionally misogynist and racist"*) and may require significant culture change.

A more diverse workforce is better able to engage with the community.

You need a sound understanding of Equality, Diversity & Inclusion issues for your interview.

You need to try and avoid outdated terminology, or you may appear to have a poor awareness of Equality, Diversity & Inclusion issues.

Cultural Reviews, HMICFRS and the Code of Ethics.

Many Fire and Rescue Services (London, as mentioned above, but also Dorset & Wiltshire, Shropshire, South Wales and others) have in recent years commissioned independent "Cultural Reviews" in response to allegations of bullying, corruption, misogyny, sexism, racism, cronyism and poor leadership. Many other services are currently undergoing, or planning for such cultural reviews.

The findings of these reviews are generally very similar, in that many of the allegations are true, and the services need to take steps to improve their workplace culture. You need to check online to see whether the service you are applying for has been subject to one of these reviews – the reports are always available online for anyone to download and are you really need to **read it thoroughly and highlight the problems identified as well as the recommendations for improvement.**

Even if your chosen fire service hasn't had a cultural review, they will be keenly aware of the issues raised in other reviews, and they will be focused on improving their culture as it is regarded as a nationwide issue.

There is an organisation called His Majesty's Inspectorate of Constabulary and Fire and Rescue Services (abbreviated to "**HMICFRS**"; often shortened to "**HMIC**" or even just "**HMI**") which is an independent body responsible for inspecting police forces (in England and Wales) and also Fire and Rescue Services (in England only, although any service can request inspections voluntarily). HMIC inspections have identified all of the above problems, and more, in the majority of fire services. Some services (Avon, Buckinghamshire, London, Gloucestershire) are either currently in, or have previously been in, a process called "Engage" which is similar to a school being placed in "Special Measures" due to concerns about their performance.

HMIC have summarised their findings in a report called *"State of Fire and Rescue: The Annual Assessment of Fire and Rescue Services in England"*. It's a lengthy report and a lot of it concerns government-level recommendations which needn't concern you too much, but one of the recommendations from the 2019 version of the report has become quite important to someone applying for a job in the fire service.

This recommendation in the 2019 report was that a "code of ethics" is established outlining expected standards of behaviour. The 2023 version of the report confirms that this recommendation has been completed and refers to "**The Core Code of Ethics**" produced by the National Fire Chiefs Council together with three other organisations (you won't need to remember who these other organisations are, but they are the Fire Standards Board, the Association of Police and Crime Commissioners and the Local Government Association).

The Core Code of Ethics is based on something called the Seven Principles of Public Life (also known as the Nolan Principles). You don't need to memorise the Nolan Principles, but it would be useful to memorise the **five ethical principles of the Core Code of Ethics**. Many fire and rescue services will ask about them directly during an interview. Or you may be asked to talk about a time when you acted in accordance with these principles. For instance, they may ask you about a time when you showed integrity, leadership, or respect for someone's dignity.

Fortunately, these principles align with the other standards and requirements of fire and rescue services, and over the coming chapters we will learn how to answer such questions.

Two other things you need to be aware of (but don't need to know all the detail of) are the enquiries into the fire service response to the Grenfell fire and the Manchester Arena bombing, both of which revealed failings in the tactics used, the equipment available, the procedures used, and particularly the way emergency services work together, amongst other things.

If you mention these things, it will be ok to say you haven't read the full reports, but you understand there's an urgent need to make improvements.

If you want to know more about the efforts being made to improve the way emergency services work together, have a look at the JESIP (Joint Emergency Services Interoperability Principles) website. This is more useful for those seeking promotion, but it wouldn't hurt for a new applicant to know about it.

KEY POINT

The **Core Code of Ethics** sets out five ethical principles:

- Putting communities first;
- Integrity;
- Dignity and respect;
- Leadership; and
- Equality, diversity and inclusion.

Use the mnemonic "PIDLE" to help you remember these.

The Code of Ethics is VERY IMPORTANT and even if you are not specifically asked about it, it will help you to mention it in your interview!

Have a think about why these principles are important in the fire service

---

You will need to be tactful about how you address these issues in an interview, and ensure you approach it with a positive attitude and use it to your advantage. So don't just say *"I can see that your organisation has a problem with racism and sexism"*. Instead say *"I can see from the recent report that you're facing challenges in terms of workplace culture, and I've noticed you've endorsed the Core Code of Ethics which is obviously a positive step and reassures me that I'll be joining a service committed to creating an inclusive workplace."*

TASK 5

Write these headings in your workbook:

INDEPENDENT REVIEWS.

Underneath this heading, write a summary of the current issues identified within UK fire and rescue services, as outlined above.

Also, look online to see if your chosen fire and rescue service has had a recent Culture Review, and if it has, look online to find the key findings and recommendations. If there are a lot of them, write down the ones that appear most important.

Record any information you can find about how your chosen service is responding to their review.

CORE CODE OF ETHICS.

Write each of the five ethical principles as a subheading, and underneath each one, write why this is important in the fire service, and why it is important that an individual firefighter abides by these principles (it's often easier to think what the consequences are if someone *doesn't* comply with these principles).

If any examples spring to mind which show how you as an individual have demonstrated behaviour in line with each principle, write a brief note to remind you of these, as they will be useful later.

Don't panic if you struggle with this – we will cover it more fully whilst producing your interview answers later.

Specific Facts About the Fire and Rescue Service You Are Applying for.

Right. This is where you can pick up some serious points for research, and it's not even difficult, which makes it all the more surprising that hardly anybody bothers. Interviewers *always* notice when a candidate has done research. Why? Because most people – stupidly – don't do it, and this makes them look lazy, unprofessional, disinterested and uncommitted.

When you interview six, eight or ten people in a day and you ask each one of them what they know about the Fire Service, and only *one* person can tell you about the day-to-day details of the job, the service's aims, ambitions, priorities, ongoing culture reviews, recent independent reports, the name of the Chief Fire Officer etc., then *that one person* is the one that sticks in your memory later when you're reviewing your notes and deciding who to employ.

Some days, particularly when I am interviewing candidates for Retained/On-Call Duty Firefighter jobs, I find it hard to stop myself from saying *"For god's sake, you're applying for a job here, and you don't even have the faintest clue what the job entails, or who we are?! Why have you even bothered coming here and wasting everyone's time?"* Don't be one of those people.

KEY POINT

If you don't make the effort to do some research, your interviewer will assume you're not really interested in the organisation or the job. If you show no interest in your potential employer or the role, then don't expect them to be interested in employing you.

Doing research shows that you have enthusiasm and motivation. Both are key attributes in the Fire and Rescue Service. Show that you've done research, and you'll **massively** improve your chance of passing the interview.

Remember, the people interviewing you aren't full-time interviewers – they are full-time Fire Service employees, involved in many different projects.

If you can name several current Fire Service activities, chances are you'll mention something your interviewers are currently, or have previously been involved with. This will strike a chord – it's a pleasant surprise when someone from outside the organisation has taken an interest in (or at least heard of) your work. Believe me. A candidate recently described a road safety campaign to me, and correctly quoted some stats about motorcycle accidents. This was a project that I had worked on personally. All the figures he quoted were correct and I could see he had made the effort to do his homework; not only was it obvious that he'd made an effort and done some research, but he came across as *enthusiastic* about the scheme and could see its benefits.

I could immediately envisage him using that enthusiasm when dealing with the public and doing good work within the organisation.

It had probably taken him less than half an hour to get the information, most likely off the service's socials. It wasn't difficult for him as we'd gone out of our way to publicise the project as widely as possible in the media, but that didn't matter at all – it showed me that he could be bothered; he could use his initiative.

TASK 6

New heading in your workbook:

THE NAME OF YOUR CHOSEN FIRE AND RESCUE SERVICE.

On this page, summarise key information from the website of the Fire Service you are applying for. You should be able to find information on the key **Aims** of the Fire Service, or **Visions** or **Ambitions**. You should also be able to find some kind of **Mission Statement**, sometimes called **Priorities** or **Values.** There may even be a document telling you exactly what the organisation's objectives and targets are for the next year or longer.

Other information you need to find:

The name of the Chief Fire Officer.
Total number of fire stations (Wholetime/On Call).
Number of employees (operational, Control and support staff).
Size of population served.
Approximate number of incidents per year (Fire, RTCs, Special Service).
Type of areas covered (coastal, urban, rural, industrial etc.)
Current high-profile campaigns*.

*The last point is a key one. You need to **FOLLOW YOUR CHOSEN FIRE SERVICE ON X, TIKTOK, FACEBOOK, INSTAGRAM ETC.**

Fire Services are getting a lot more social media-savvy in their efforts to get their messages across. If you follow them on social media, you will receive updates of all the things that they really want the public to know, and these are things you should definitely know in an interview.

Even if you are a technophobe, it's not that hard to get into social media. You may also get to hear about the latest incidents this way, which will give you a good idea of the reactive work.

We will refer back to this information when producing answers to specific questions in Part 5.

Speak to Employees for the Inside Story

If you have followed all of the above steps, then you will have enough information in your notebook to deliver a good response to any questions about your understanding of the Fire and Rescue Service. You will have picked up all of the key messages that the Fire Service wants the pubic to think about.

There is another step you can take though, if you want to take you answer to the next level, as there are some things that you won't get to know about no matter how thoroughly you search the Fire Service websites or social media feeds. These are the things that are not necessarily very shiny or positive, the things that the Fire Service may not want to shout about. The "warts and all" stuff. To get the lowdown on this, you need to speak to people in the job.

Go to your local wholetime fire station, introduce yourself and ask if you could speak to the Officer in Charge for 10-15 mins. They may pass you along to someone else able to help you, that's fine. Mention that you are going for an interview and say that you're doing as much research as you can. People actually do this, and Fire Service personnel understand why, so you won't look weird or get told to go away (unless you're unlucky enough to get an extremely negative and grumpy watch). They may be busy and ask you to come back at a more convenient time which is understandable, especially if you turn up during shift-change or during an exercise or drill (or worse still, during dinner).

You could even show them this paragraph if you like. Basically, you've found out all the official stuff about the Fire Service from the website and social media. You need to know about the challenges facing the Fire Service. Every Fire Service has its problems, and they are usually related to a combination of the following factors:

Annual leave, new procedures, new or ineffective equipment, new or defective ICT systems, new duties, higher expectations, changes to shift systems, attacks on pensions, pay-rises not matching inflation, the possibility of strikes, culture reviews and independent reports, workers being brought in to cover during strikes (very sensitive), an ageing workforce serving an ageing population, cuts to staff numbers, cuts to appliances, station closures, budget cuts, skills fade due to declining call numbers, on-call availability, defective equipment, high rise procedures/evacuation, changes to contracts, too many demands on their time (completing online and in-person training, often on topics not directly related to the job, recording the training), and usually low morale caused by some or all of the above.

It's important to get an impression of the challenges facing the Fire Service from the perspective of a person working on an actual wholetime fire station. Why? So you can give a more full and rounded answer to any questions about your understanding of the Fire Service and seem less naïve or robotic. Whilst you're at the fire station, you should take the opportunity to find out the ground-level perspective on the other things you've found out about during your research.

I've specifically recommended visiting a *wholetime* fire station for a reason. Wholetime firefighters perform the role as their primary/only occupation. They spend their entire working life based at the fire station and often know the organisation far better than their on-call counterparts who typically a much smaller amount of time there. Also, if you're applying to be a wholetime firefighter, then it makes sense to speak to serving wholetime firefighters for the lowdown. An on-call firefighter may focus on issues relating to the on-call duty system such as rotas and clashes with their main employment. You could still visit your local retained station if that's what you're aiming for.

As an aside, I remember being asked in my Fire Service interview *"What was the most recent thing you had to learn?"* I was able to use hose-running (unravelling and laying out a 70mm fire hose) as an example as I had visited my local station to practice this part of the (old) physical test. It must have impressed the interviewer as I got the job! Feel free to mention your station visit in your interview – it will help to show that you are keen.

TASK 7

Visit a fire station. Ask the Watch Manager (or Sub Officer in London Fire Brigade) if you could have a chat about the Fire Service. Answer the following questions on a page headed **STATION VISIT**:

- What is the mix of calls they attend, and how many?
- What kind of Risk Reduction work do they carry out?
- What are the biggest challenges facing the Fire Service/station?
- Have there been any recent independent reviews/reports?
- What is being done to address these challenges?

Whilst you're there, it won't hurt to ask for interview tips. They may have a probationer on the watch who could give you an idea of what questions they were asked in their recent interview.

You should end up with quite a bit of information which we're going to use when composing interview answers later on.

If your chosen Fire Service is a long way away, or if you just don't like the idea of visiting a Fire Station, there are other ways to glean this kind of information. You can try and get in touch with someone from that Fire Service online – search for *"Fire Service Forum"*. There are a few on the internet/Facebook etc. You can register/join and ask the above questions; they're a friendly and helpful bunch and surprisingly open with information (people on forums are often more open as they can use pseudonyms). It would be wise if you didn't use your real name either, just in case you annoy or get into an argument with your future interviewer!

TIP: Station personnel are often quite willing to help you with your preparation for the Physical and Practical Stage of the recruitment process. Ask if anyone is able to advise you on things like the ladder lift/dummy drag/equipment carry/confined space test etc. They may ask you to come back another time and set up a practice session for you. As well as being useful in a practical sense, your interviewer is likely to be impressed that you have made the effort to do this.

PART 2 – SUMMARY

There was a fair bit of donkeywork involved in that chapter – well done if you completed it all. The work you have done here will stand you in good stead for the interview.

You should now have a pretty good idea of how the Fire Service works in general including the key laws that govern it, as well as knowing some key facts about your chosen Fire Service such as its size, the area it covers, how many stations there are, who is in charge etc.

You should also know a lot about the work it undertakes, both reactive and preventative, as well as the challenges it faces.

You'll also have the mission statement, vision and values if your Fire Service has these things.

On top of all this you will now have a good grasp of the concepts of Equality, Equity and Diversity; how well the makeup of your chosen Fire Service reflects its local community; and what it is doing to address any discrepancies.

Read through what you've written so far. Highlight the key information.

Remember, the interview is a competitive process. Most of your competitors haven't done any of this research. You're already in the lead.

Now Let's Talk About *You!*

Some self-reflection

Ok. So far, it's all been about the Fire and Rescue Service. Obviously though, you won't be spending the whole interview reciting facts about incidents, fire engines, legislation etc. Chances are, you'll be talking about *yourself* for over 90% of the interview, which is why the majority of this book focuses on *you.* In the next chapter we will be looking at your experiences to see where your strengths and weaknesses are. With a bit of work, we will improve your areas of weakness and make a solid plan to enable you to show off your strengths in a way that makes you look like ideal Fire and Rescue Service material.

Before we get into the nuts and bolts of the specific attributes the Fire and Rescue Service look for in an interview, you need to do a bit of reflection.

Don't spend any more than 15 minutes on this next task – that's less than 2 mins per bullet-point. Don't freak out if you struggle to think of examples or if the best ones you can think of seem weak. Write what you can. This is just a preliminary exercise to get you thinking; you're not committing to using any of this in the interview. We will address any weaknesses in a while.

TASK 8

Under a new heading "**MY EXPERIENCE**" in your notebook, list the best possible examples of a time when you...

- Worked as part of a team, preferably whilst motivating others
- Worked independently or with minimal supervision
- Devised a plan or solved a problem
- Overcame significant difficulties or challenges
- Showed integrity, sensitivity or took account of people's differences
- Coped with a high-pressure or time-critical situation
- Dealt with change
- Improved or developed yourself
- Helped someone else develop
- Showed awareness of mental health issues

They do not have to be work-related. They can be connected with hobbies, sports, clubs, home renovations, life in general, anything as long as it fits. Some of your examples may relate to more than one of the above questions.

Ideally you should be thinking about reasonably significant and challenging experiences here. Doing a Sudoku puzzle isn't good enough for "Solving a Problem".

If you found that easy, you've either got some good experience or you're deluded about how good you are. We will soon find out. Whichever one it is, the following sections should help you to improve your evidence and also help you to identify and develop some new material. It's also worth highlighting what you feel are your best and weakest pieces of experience and labelling them for later.

Next, we need to establish what criteria your chosen Fire Service uses in the interview. It will be one of two.

PQAs or NFCC Leadership Framework?

This section talks about the two main methods used by UK Fire and Rescue Services to evaluate candidates during an interview. They are:

Personal Qualities and Attributes (PQAs) – A system introduced in 2009, and still in use in many regions.

NFCC* Leadership Framework – Introduced in 2019, this system is designed to replace the PQAs and is gradually being adopted nationally.

You need to find out which system your chosen service is using.

1. It *should* be clearly stated in the documentation sent out during the application process. If not;
2. Check their website's recruitment page for a candidate information pack;
3. Ring the HR/Recruitment department and ask politely, *"In your recruitment interviews, will you be using the PQAs or the NFCC Leadership Framework?"* It's not a secret and they should tell you straight away;
4. Enquire on a Fire Service internet forum – there are a lot of knowledgeable and helpful people; or
5. Ask someone in the job. Be careful though, as a lot of firefighters naturally lose interest in the recruitment process once they are in the job, and they may give you outdated information.

TASK 9

Find out whether your chosen Fire and Rescue Service has switched to the NFCC Leadership Framework or is still using the old PQA system.

If in doubt / they say they use another system, use the **NFCC Framework**.

You only need to read either *"Part 3 – PQAs"*; or "Part 4 – NFCC Leadership Framework" depending on the information you obtained in Task 9.

*National Fire Chiefs' Council

Part 3 – Personal Qualities and Attributes (PQAs)

OK, so you have established that your chosen Fire and Rescue Service is still using the PQA system – no problem. This next bit is going to take a while, but it will be well worth it – it is one of the most important parts of your preparation.

Quick reminder – if your chosen Fire Service is using the NFCC Framework in their interviews, or if they say they're using another system, or if you just can't find out, skip this section, and move to Part 4.

In this section we're going to look at the qualities you need in order to be a Firefighter, and which of these qualities your interviewer is most likely to be looking for in you.

Later, when we look at which qualities you've actually *got*, it should be obvious if you have any shortfalls. Once that's done, we will move on to fixing any problems identified. Stay with the programme – there's logic and experience behind this!

This may be the first time you've ever come across the term *Personal Qualities and Attributes* or *PQA's*. Well, you're going to be hearing a lot more about them.

In a nutshell, **Personal Qualities and Attributes (PQAs)** are a way for interviewers to measure your *potential* to carry out the role you're applying for.

It would be unreasonable to expect someone applying to be a firefighter to know how to do the job in advance, so it wouldn't be fair if an interviewer started asking you about high-rise / breathing apparatus procedures before you've received any training.

Instead, you are assessed to see if you have the *potential* to carry out the role. These PQAs cover your ability to work with others, to act appropriately in conflict situations, to be part of a team and to communicate effectively. Because they measure your behaviour, they are also known as Behavioural Indicators [Source – IPDS website].

Two very important things for you to understand: Firstly, when a Fire and Rescue Service conducts interviews using the PQAs, your score is directly related to how well you can show that you hit the PQAs. Some Fire and Rescue Services have referred to "Competencies", which are essentially PQAs with another name.

Secondly, most Fire and Rescue Services use the "experiential" or "evidence-based" format for the interview questions.

These are the kind of questions that begin with *"Tell us about a time when..."* or *"Can you give an example of how you..."* What this means is you won't get any points for saying *"I'm a great team-player."* or *"I'm fantastic at solving problems."*

You need to be able to *prove* you've got these qualities, using specific examples of real-world experiences, and whilst doing so, you need to make sure you're hitting the criteria of the PQA/s being tested by that question.

KEY POINT

Many Fire and Rescue Services will seek to assess your potential to do the job by comparing your behaviour against a set of criteria known as *Personal Qualities and Attributes (PQAs)*.

Interviewers will mark your performance against a list of PQAs, giving you points for how well you meet the requirements.

You need to learn the PQAs now, so that later on when it comes to selecting and writing and your answers, you know what you are aiming for and you can word your responses as effectively as possible, based on the criteria being assessed.

If you have received an applicant's information pack, scrutinise it for information about the interview – it may provide clues as to the nature of the questions and the time allotted for answers.

We jumped ahead a bit there deliberately, to give you some idea of why we are about to focus so much effort on PQAs.

Otherwise, you may think we're obsessing over them unnecessarily; believe me, this section is very necessary. It's essential that you are able to prove you've got the right PQAs in the interview, and to help you do this, we're going to look at the PQAs very closely.

They are the backbone of your preparation, and you need to pay serious attention to this bit.

We are going to go analyse each PQA in turn, but here are the nine individual headings to give you a feeling of what the interviewer will be looking for:

1. **Working with Others** *
2. **Commitment to Diversity & Integrity** *
3. **Commitment to Excellence** *
4. **Commitment to Development** *
5. **Effective Communication**
6. **Openness to Change**
7. **Problem Solving**
8. **Confidence & Resilience**
9. **Situational Awareness**

If you were to look up the PQAs on a Fire Service or Government ("Skills for Justice") website, you will see them in a different sequence, but I have listed them in order of how often they come up in interviews.

* According to the *'PQA Interview Technical Manual'*, only PQAs **1** to **4** from the above list should ever be formally tested in an interview, with PQA **5** being assessed by looking at your verbal communication skills during the interview overall. However, I have occasionally seen PQAs **6, 7 & 8** tested at interview.

In my experience, Situational Awareness is tested very, very rarely at the interview stage. If you are stuck for time, you could take a small risk and not spend much (or any) time preparing for that particular PQA.

The PQA section that follows is a combination of the official definitions plus the descriptions given in the Behaviourally Anchored Rating Scales (**BARS**), which are essentially the interviewers' marking sheet. I have also added my own professional interpretation, which is the distillation of many years of working in this field.

The PQAs supposedly enable interviewers to assess a member of the public with no Fire Service experience, and yet they refer to tasks such as use of breathing apparatus, which is slightly nonsensical. I've re-worded some of these parts to make them more useful to someone not currently in the Fire Service.

Remember, the PQAs are listed in this book order of importance in terms of how often they crop up in interviews. PQAs 1 to 4 are the most important to you so you may want to focus more on them than on the rest.

NOTE FOR EXISTING FIRE SERVICE EMPLOYEES

(If you have never worked in a uniformed role in the Fire and Rescue Service, you can just ignore this box, and don't let it confuse you!)

If you are <u>wholetime</u> and preparing for a <u>promotion</u> process, then you should use the following section in conjunction with the relevant Supervisory/Middle Manager BARS document, as this includes additional PDAs such as the *"Planning and Implementing"* PQA which doesn't feature in the Firefighter PQAs/initial selection process.

If you are an existing <u>on call</u> firefighter preparing for a <u>wholetime</u> interview, you should complete the next task using *original* PQA definitions (available online or from your intranet or HR department). The reason for this is the original wording of the PQAs incudes references to Fire and Rescue Service activities, and you *will* be able to use Fire and Rescue Service experiences in your interview if you work for a Fire Service already.

TASK 10

This is a big one, and it will take a while, but it's worth it.

At the top of the next 9 pages of your workbook, write the PQAs in the same order that they have just been introduced, so you have a sheet for each PQA.

(If you're already in the Fire Service and preparing for a promotion interview, you need to include the additional PQAs i.e. *"Planning and Implementing".*)

Next, read through the descriptions of the PQAs provided in the following pages. **Read them thoroughly, so you actually take them in and understand them. No skim-reading!**

Once you've read each PQA:

- Copy down the important information relating to each PQA on the corresponding page in your workbook. Include the key words and phrases and the summary.
- Describe each PQA, *in your own words*.
- Note down any activities, experiences or jobs you can think of that needed the qualities described by each PQA – just a brief heading is needed – something like *"Coaching Under-11's Football"* on your 'Working with Others' page, for example.
- Write down any positive personality traits under the most relevant PQA. If you're proud of your timekeeping, say, note down any examples of when you have shown this quality.

This isn't just a mindless memorisation technique; we need you to get these PQAs firmly lodged in your mind as soon as possible – they're going to count for a great deal.

NOTE: You will never gain points for spouting PQAs in an interview, but *knowing what they are will enable you to produce far more relevant answers,* worded in the correct style. Having the right words in your vocabulary and the right concepts in your mind will help you think and talk in the right kind of language during the interview.

Personal Qualities and Attributes (PQAs)

PQA 1 – Working with Others

Works effectively with others both within own organisation and in the wider community

- Works effectively with all team-members according to defined role, adjusting his/her role in accordance with instructions and changing circumstances.
- Proactively generates positive working relationships, building rapport with a range of people both internally (your company/organisation) and externally (community groups/other organisations).
- Concerned about the wider team and aware of shared objectives, as well as those of his/her immediate work-team.
- Sensitive to the feelings and well-being of others and takes action to support them (e.g. able to reassure and calm people in stressful situations; refocuses people on specific tasks when they are anxious or overloaded).
- Presents an approachable and positive image of self and their organisation to external agencies and the wider community, irrespective of individual differences.

Behaviourally Anchored Ratings Scales (BARS) Description

- Builds rapport and works well with all team members.
- Proactively builds relationships with those internally and looks for opportunities to involve others.
- Actively looks for opportunities to get to know the local community (e.g. volunteers to deliver presentations at various local community groups).
- Continually looks to help, support and reassure others (e.g. recognises when team members need support and offers help without prompting).
- Inspires others through their motivation, encouraging others to feel part of the team.
- Consistently cares for self and cares for others.

THE "WORKING WITH OTHERS" PQA

TRANSLATED INTO PLAIN ENGLISH:

One of the most important skills of a firefighter is the ability to work as a part of a team. This is just as important at an incident as it is back at the station where you all have to get along together for long periods. To work well in a team, you need to be able to follow instructions, know what your role is and how you fit in with the other team members. An understanding of the roles of other team members and how to adjust to changes is essential.

You need to be able to involve people and groups from outside the Fire and Rescue Service too, so you mustn't focus entirely on those within your immediate team.

You also need to be mindful of the feelings and needs of others and be able to respond effectively to support them. Mental health is a crucial consideration in the Fire and Rescue Service as traumatic incidents can have a profound and lasting effect on people's emotional wellbeing.

KEY WORDS: *WELL-BALANCED, CARING, APPROACHABLE, ENTHUSIASTIC, ENCOURAGING, SUPPORTIVE, TRUSTING, INSPIRING, MOTIVATING, EMPATHETIC, SENSITIVE, CREDIBLE, ENERGETIC, PROACTIVE, POSITIVE, PERSUASIVE.*

THIS IS ONE OF THE FOUR KEY PQAS OFFICIALLY TESTED AT INTERVIEW

Understands and respects diversity and adopts a fair and ethical approach to others.

- Is concerned to treat people fairly and ethically (e.g. completes work according to same high standards regardless of individual differences).
- Recognises the importance of an awareness of the community and understands its needs (e.g. is aware and respectful of differing cultures and backgrounds).
- Recognises and has respect for others' backgrounds, views, values and beliefs (including religious beliefs).
- Maintains an open approach with others, taking account of, and accepting, individual differences such as age, ethnicity, gender, religious beliefs, social background, disability, sexual orientation and physical appearance.
- Is committed to the Fire and Rescue Service values and actively promotes them (e.g. challenges inappropriate behaviour).
- Is honest when working with others and accepts accountability for own actions (e.g. quickly takes responsibility for own mistakes; respects the need for confidentiality; is trusted to enter others' homes).
- Proactively challenges unacceptable behaviour inconsistent with Fire and Rescue Service values, stating own and organisation's position clearly (e.g. when over-hearing a colleague use inappropriate language).

Behaviourally Anchored Ratings Scales (BARS) Description

Diversity

- Seeks and respects the views of others.
- Proactively maintains a knowledge of community needs.
- Has time for everyone and is always fair to others.
- Fully accepting of others' views and individual differences.
- Consistently accommodates the needs and views of others.

<u>Integrity</u>

- Fully compliant with confidentiality policies.
- Fully committed to Fire Service values.
- Educates and influences others to promote diversity and integrity in the workplace.
- Addresses inappropriate behaviour proactively.
- Always admits own mistakes, takes corrective action so as to minimise the impact on others.

THE "COMMITMENT TO DIVERSITY AND INTEGRITY" PQA

TRANSLATED INTO PLAIN ENGLISH:

As a Firefighter, you will be expected to deliver first-class service to each and every member of the community regardless of their background (refer back to the Equality & Diversity section for the 9 Protected Characteristics; also, the Equality Act). <u>This does not mean treating everyone the same</u>. This means making an effort to understand differences and treat people fairly, with due consideration to their needs and respect for their dignity

There is no place in the Fire Service for discrimination or bigotry. You are expected to challenge unacceptable behaviour when you encounter it. Just ignoring a colleague's racist jokes isn't good enough.

Honesty is a key trait in a Firefighter, and this includes identifying your own mistakes, owning-up to them, rectifying them and apologising if necessary.

<u>KEY WORDS:</u> *RESPECTFUL, FAIR, ETHICAL, TOLERANT, HONEST, LIBERAL, TRUSTWORTHY, CONSIDERATE, COMPASSIONATE, EMPATHETIC, UNDERSTANDING, PATIENT, PRINCIPLED, CONSCIENCIOUS, TRUTHFUL.*

THIS IS ONE OF THE FOUR KEY PQAS OFFICIALLY TESTED AT INTERVIEW

KEY POINT

Note that the Fire and Rescue Service PQA talks about to *Commitment to...*

*Diversity and **Integrity***

Whereas the Equalities Act refers to...

*Diversity and **Equality***

This doesn't mean you can ignore Equality issues; they're all lumped-in with Diversity in the Fire Service.

What it does mean, though, is that, if you are ever asked to prove your Commitment to Diversity and Integrity, you don't always need to focus on the Diversity aspect, so you don't necessarily have to go down the *"9 Protected Characteristics"* route.

If you have better evidence relating to *integrity*, for instance something demonstrating honesty, trustworthiness and owning-up to your mistakes, then that may be a good option to consider, rather than using a weak piece of *diversity* evidence.

As always though, pay very close attention to the wording of the question to ensure you are answering it properly.

Adopts a conscientious and proactive approach to work to achieve and maintain excellent standards.

- Continually looks to improve standards of working and offers suggestions as necessary (e.g. provides feedback concerning new or existing work practices to influence change or improve performance).
- Approaches work proactively and efficiently both with routine tasks and when under pressure.
- Adopts a conscientious approach to work (e.g. checks work to ensure all tasks completed correctly and with due attention to detail; maintains appropriate levels of personal fitness).
- Completes work using appropriate procedures (e.g. refrains from taking unsafe short-cuts).
- Completes work as instructed without being reminded constantly.
- Is clear about the role of the firefighter and operates within agreed levels of authority and accountability (e.g. does not take action outside own level of control without seeking confirmation). *
- Demonstrates a commitment to the work of the Fire and Rescue Service, viewing its role as socially important. *

Although these last two points both refer to the Fire Service, it should be possible for you to hit these criteria without any experience of actually working within a Fire Service, thanks to all the research you did in Part 2.

Behaviourally Anchored Ratings Scales (BARS) Description

- Is known for making regular suggestions and finding faults to improve standards of working.
- Takes a proactive approach to work and completes their work to a high standard.
- Proactively helps; asks if work needs to be done.
- Follows all the correct rules and procedures, will not cut corners unless doing so could improve a situation and he/she has permission.
- Sets an example; constantly monitors themselves and others to maintain high standards (e.g. encourages others to work to high standards).
- Standards of work exceed the expected requirement.
- Keen to promote the role of Firefighter in the local community.

THE "COMMITMENT TO EXCELLENCE" PQA

TRANSLATED INTO PLAIN ENGLISH:

Firefighters are expected to be able to follow instructions and complete tasks without being told twice, even in high-pressure situations.

A firefighter should continually assess their work to ensure it is of the highest standard and also identify any ways of improving the way things are done.

It is important that a Firefighter doesn't "*freelance*" and do things they are not supposed to be doing, however you do need the ability to adapt when necessary, without continually seeking approval. To do the job well, a Firefighter needs to appreciate the importance of the role.

KEY WORDS: *CONSCIENTIOUS, PROACTIVE, ROLE-MODEL, POSITIVE, SAFE, HIGH STANDARDS, EFFICIENT, CALM, THOROUGH, FIT, CAREFUL, METICULOUS, RELIABLE, INDEPENDENT, SEEKS IMPROVEMENT.*

THIS IS ONE OF THE FOUR KEY PQAS OFFICIALLY TESTED AT INTERVIEW

Committed to and able to develop self and others.

- Proactively reviews own performance using a variety of sources including seeking feedback from others (e.g. uses appraisals and personal development reviews to inform development).
- Identifies development needs in own knowledge, skills and understanding and takes action to improve (e.g. requests specific training as appropriate; makes a point of keeping up to date with changes in technology/work processes; recognises that own fitness levels need to be improved).
- Learns from a wide range of situations experienced by self or others (e.g. increases understanding about other organisations following meetings).
- Able to learn and retain a large amount of job relevant information, delivered both verbally and in writing, as part of an initial training course and ongoing development (e.g. work processes and standards).
- Actively encourages and supports others to continuously improve (e.g. updates colleagues concerning new information; participates in a mentoring programme to support new members of staff).
- Motivates self to keep relevant knowledge up to date.

Behaviourally Anchored Ratings Scales (BARS) Description

- Constantly reviews own performance; actively seeks feedback on own performance from a range of sources.
- Knows and seeks out the latest information relevant to his/her immediate and wider role from a variety of sources (e.g. internet, visits, experienced colleagues etc.)
- Constantly seeks to educate and improve others; is enthusiastic about supporting the development of others.
- Able to gather and apply a large amount of job-related information from training situations.
- Develops self over and above the level required for the role.

- Seeks out and uses a range of methods to develop self during training and in everyday job situations (e.g. will question experienced team members to extend own learning).

THE "COMMITMENT TO DEVELOPMENT" PQA

TRANSLATED INTO PLAIN ENGLISH:

To be a good firefighter you must continuously assess your own skills and knowledge against what is required, and where necessary, produce appropriate action plans to address your deficiencies.

As well as self-assessment, you can use appraisals and instigate conversations with other team members to get feedback on where you are falling short or where you have development needs.

Many different situations can be used as opportunities to improve your effectiveness in the role; action plans may include a combination of incidents, drills, simulations, procedural documents, training courses, lectures, Q&A sessions, online training etc.

A good firefighter is keen to share new information with the team and support the development of others.

KEY WORDS: *PROACTIVE, ENTHUSIASTIC, CONSCIENTIOUS, MOTIVATED, ENCOURAGING, SUPPORTIVE, KEEN LEARNER, GOOD MEMORY, REFLECTIVE AND HONEST ABOUT OWN ABILITIES, CURIOUS, MENTORING.*

THIS IS ONE OF THE FOUR KEY PQAS OFFICIALLY TESTED AT INTERVIEW

Communicates effectively both orally and in writing.

- Communicates verbal messages clearly, concisely and at a level appropriate to the audience so that messages are understood regardless of individual differences.
- Is sensitive to the needs of the audience and tailors communication in response to feedback (e.g. able to convey safety information without causing undue distress).
- Constantly alert for new information and listens actively to ensure accurate understanding (e.g. using appropriate body language, or by asking questions).
- Asks appropriate questions and checks understanding to ensure all messages received and sent are clearly understood (e.g. asks colleague to repeat message).
- Communicates effectively with both small and large groups.
- Presents messages in a way that promotes understanding (e.g. uses slides, videos, other visual aids appropriately during presentations and group discussions; engages with the audience).
- Writes clear, basic and appropriate information or messages that are understood by the recipient (e.g. completes forms correctly). *[The original document refers to completing Breathing Apparatus boards, but think "attention to detail" if you haven't worked in the Fire Service.]*

Behaviourally Anchored Ratings Scales (BARS) Description

Oral Communication

- Speaks with clarity and confidence to all people in all situations.
- Actively listens throughout interactions.
- Always adapts the style, content and complexity of messages to suit the audience and the situation.
- Always checks that his/her messages are understood.

- Can engage all audiences and makes presentations interesting, interactive and engaging.
- Is able to comfortably deliver a wide variety of presentations; seeks opportunities to do so.

Written Communication

- Writes messages with clarity and accuracy; messages contain all relevant information.

THE "EFFECTIVE COMMUNCATION" PQA

TRANSLATED INTO PLAIN ENGLISH:

There is not a dedicated 'communication' question in most Fire Service interviews. Instead, you gain marks based on the clarity with which you present your answers.

Communication is key in the Fire Service as it affects the success of much of the work. You need to communicate well under pressure, in time-critical situations, over the din of sirens, fire alarms, revving diesel engines, over the radio and through muffled breathing apparatus.

You need the patience and sensitivity to convey safety information to children, the elderly, those with dementia, disabilities or no English language.

Communication is as much about listening as it is about speaking, and you always need to check that your message has been understood.

If you have to use acronyms or jargon, explain them for the benefit of the panel – this shows you are able to consider your audience.

KEY WORDS: *CLEAR, CONCISE, SENSITIVE, LISTENS, ADAPTABLE, STRUCTURED, EMPATHETIC, CONSISTENT, ADAPTABLE, ALERT, OPEN, CONSIDERATE, ENGAGING, CONFIDENT*

This PQA should be tested by looking at your verbal skills during interview, but it has been known for candidates to be asked specific questions on Effective Communication in past interviews.

Is open to change and actively seeks to support it.

- Demonstrates an understanding of the need for progress within the Fire and Rescue Service (e.g. explains the reasons for new working practices to colleagues absent from briefings).
- Accepts change both within the Fire and Rescue Service and in their own role and adapts effectively (e.g. willingly participates in community fire safety activities).
- Is aware of the impact of changes to the Fire and Rescue Service on their role (e.g. understands changes to working practices).
- Identifies ways of supporting change and takes action where possible (e.g. is proactive in learning new tasks or ways of working).

Behaviourally Anchored Ratings Scales (BARS) Description

- Actively promotes progress with colleagues.
- Is always willing to try new methods when asked to do so.
- Aware of the main changes affecting their role and the Fire Service as a whole.
- Proactively shares ideas, explains them and provides solutions.

THE "OPENNESS TO CHANGE" PQA

TRANSLATED INTO PLAIN ENGLISH:

As Heraclitus said, *"Everything changes, and nothing stands still"*. This is especially true in the Fire and Rescue Service.

As a Firefighter you will be expected to continually update your skills and knowledge to keep abreast of new risks, equipment, procedures and scenarios. Don't expect to rely on anyone else to keep you up-to-speed though, as you will be responsible for maintaining your own competencies. Yes, you will be programmed onto certain courses to ensure you remain "in compliance" with Breathing Apparatus, Trauma and RTC skills, but a good Firefighter takes the initiative in "horizon-scanning" to ensure they are prepared for the future and not lacking any essential skills or knowledge.

A Firefighter transferring from a rural to an urban station should identify a need for – and ensure they receive – additional High-Rise training whereas someone transferring the other way may consider Large Animal Rescue, for instance. The risks associated with an ageing population may prompt a good Firefighter to consider what additional skills they require to cope, for example dementia awareness training.

The important thing to demonstrate in the interview is that you are not just *prepared to accept* change, but that you are *keen to drive* change and you *seek opportunities* to change things for the better.

KEY WORDS: *INITIATIVE, FLEXIBLE, PROACTIVE, ADAPTABLE, FORWARD-THINKING, ENCOURAGING, POSITIVE, OPEN-MINDED, INNOVATIVE*

This is not one of the four key PQAs officially tested at interview, but many Fire and Rescue Services have chosen to ask candidates specific questions on Openness to Change in past interviews.

Understands, recalls, applies and adapts relevant information in an organised, safe and systematic way.

- Able to recall and apply relevant job-related information and procedures whilst completing work tasks, does not take information at face value when making a decision (e.g. does not assume that all information provided is necessarily accurate).
- Applies, and, if necessary, adapts current procedures and practices and to take account of a changing environment and to minimise risk.
- Generates more than one solution to a problem and evaluates which one is best (e.g. in deciding how best communicate a message to a particular group).
- Considers immediate and wider objectives and implications (e.g. health and safety) to plan ahead to complete tasks in most efficient and safe way.
- Prioritises, plans and completes tasks in a logical and systematic manner despite conflicting information (e.g. able to manage own actions during time-critical situations).
- Able to understand, interpret and manipulate basic numerical information (e.g. in dials, tables, charts) and use basic arithmetical calculations correctly to apply task procedures (e.g. able to interpret gauge readings to establish quantities).

Behaviourally Anchored Ratings Scales (BARS) Description

- Can instantly gather the correct information to apply within a given situation.
- Is able to question or correct others' approaches to
- tasks due to his/her extensive knowledge.
- Consistently adapts knowledge to deal with new circumstances, generating a number of solutions and deciding on the one that maximises effectiveness and minimises risk.

- Prioritises actions to maximise efficiency and safety, taking account of the immediate and wider situation.
- Deals with complex problems in a logical, systematic way.
- Competent and confident when dealing with the full range of numerical information, with exceptional accuracy

THE "PROBLEM SOLVING" PQA

TRANSLATED INTO PLAIN ENGLISH:

You are at house fire, in breathing apparatus. You're instructed to force the front door to fight a fire in a rear kitchen. Whilst making your way through the hall in thick smoke you hear screams from upstairs. A second team is outside, getting ready to search upstairs but they will be a couple of minutes yet.

Do you fight the fire as instructed or go upstairs to search for the occupants whilst a fire rages downstairs? What radio message do you send?

You need to be able to assess several options and select the one that is most appropriate for you, your team and for others. You may need to make quick, important decisions based on incomplete or conflicting information. You can't always achieve everything you want to, so you need to able to prioritise your objectives and explain your reasoning afterwards.

The important thing is not to be indecisive. You need to make quick decisions based upon consideration of all the facts available, which may include some assumptions. You should generate multiple solutions and be able to justify your decision.

KEY WORDS: *ANALYTICAL, LOGICAL, SYSTEMATIC, PERCEPTIVE, ACCURATE, EFFICIENT, PROBING, ADAPTABLE, EFFICIENT, PLANNING, QUESTIONING, KNOWLEDGABLE, NUMERATE, METHODICAL, SYSTEMATIC*

This is not one of the four key PQAs officially tested at interview, but many Fire and Rescue Services have chosen to ask candidates specific questions on Problem Solving in past interviews.

Maintains a confident and resilient attitude in highly challenging situations.

- Remains in control of own emotions during stressful situations (e.g. does not panic and considers risk).
- Concentrates on the task despite pressure (e.g. pressure of time, noise, conflicting information and tasks).
- Challenges or questions others constructively to achieve more effective outcomes.
- Retains confidence in own ability or convictions despite setbacks (e.g. after a presentation is received poorly).

Behaviourally Anchored Ratings Scales (BARS) Description

Confidence

- Always rational and in control of their emotions during emergency or challenging situations, whilst supporting and reassuring others under stress.
- Can always concentrate on the task in hand.
- Quickly and immediately prioritises actions appropriately in stressful, time-critical situations without direct prompting, even when dealing with multiple-sources of information.
- Always assertive without being confrontational or submissive even if constantly challenged.

Resilience

- Always makes an appropriate, constructive challenge to clarify ambiguous or unsafe instructions or to challenge inappropriate views.
- Reflects on challenging situations and always looks to improve and commit to a higher standard of work.

THE "CONFIDENCE & RESILIENCE" PQA

TRANSLATED INTO PLAIN ENGISH:

A Firefighter has to be able to deal with a wide range of challenging situations without losing their cool or allowing their emotions to take over. You may be confronted with angry or confused members of the public whose loved ones are missing or dying; they may be under the influence of alcohol or other drugs; they may be aggressive or irrational as a result of head injuries, shock or mental illness. You may have to explain to confrontational police officers why you are closing a motorway during rush-hour. You will often find yourself surrounded by people filming you on their phones whilst you deal with these situations. You will need to remain unflustered even if you make a mistake.

You need to be able to assert yourself without escalating the situation; you need to stay focused on the job at hand regardless of the amount of stress and pressure you are under. Afterwards, you will need to assess your performance and seek ways to improve.

Also, linking back to *Diversity and Integrity*, you need to be able to stand up and challenge people's unacceptable comments and behaviour, regardless of how uncomfortable this feels.

KEY WORDS: *RATIONAL, CONFIDENT, UNFLUSTERED, CONTROLLED, CALM, ASSERTIVE, FOCUSED, QUESTIONING.*

This is not one of the four key PQAs officially tested at interview, but many Fire and Rescue Services have chosen to ask candidates specific questions on Confidence and Resilience in past interviews.

Maintains an active awareness of the environment to promote safe and effective working.

- Constantly checks the environment and takes action to ensure safe working (e.g. looks for and assesses risks to safety of self and others.
- Has awareness of a range of safety related information without becoming unduly focused on any one piece of information (e.g. considers full range of factors, such as location of other team members in a high-risk situation).
- Provides timely and accurate information to confirm progress and outcomes against objectives (e.g. keeps team informed of changing circumstances).
- Able to judge space and distance within three dimensions and time to perform tasks safely and effectively (e.g. able to judge space and distance to work with ladders).

Behaviourally Anchored Ratings Scales (BARS) Description

- Remains constantly alert to the environment for all hazards, reports them and takes preventative action without being prompted.
- Consistently uses equipment within its limitations and capabilities.
- Consistently monitors their personal fitness level and takes action to prevent poor health, fitness and hygiene.
- Consistently operates within agreed level of authority and responsibility.
- Consistently provides records that are in the agreed format, accurate, complete, legible and accessible to authorised users.
- Consistently acts with relevant urgency to minimise any risks.
- Consistently returns and secures resources to their correct location and report defects and deficiencies.
- Never compromises availability for operational response. *[This one is useful for On-Call/Retained personnel preparing for interviews, but no use if you have never worked in the Fire Service.]*

THE "SITUATIONAL AWARENESS" PQA

TRANSLATED INTO PLAIN ENLGLISH:

A Firefighter needs to be aware of the changing and developing hazards and risks around them at an incident and how these factors affect their safety and the safety of others.

A wall that looks like it may collapse, an open pit in the ground, gas cylinders, hypodermic needles, a colleague not adhering to the relevant procedures, an aggressive casualty... there are many kinds of hazards, and you need to be able to recognise them, deal with them and tell others about them in good time.

You need to look after the equipment and maintain accurate testing records. The most important piece of equipment is your own mind and body, and you need to have a proper health and fitness regime including nutrition, strength and cardio training to ensure you are fit to do the job.

KEY WORDS: *VIGILANT, PERCEPTIVE, ACCURATE, SAFE, PRACTICAL, RESPONSBLE, ALERT, FIT, HEALTHY, COORDINATED*

This is not one of the four key PQAs officially tested at interview, and it is very rare for a Fire and Rescue Service to ask candidates a specific question on Situational Awareness during an interview.

So, that's all the PQAs. Go back to the Task 10 workbox and ensure you have completed it fully. For each PQA you should now have a summary with key words and phrases, a description of it in your own words, a list of examples of times when you have demonstrated the qualities described, and any key attributes that you think you may have which tally with the PQAs.

This task may have been difficult and time-consuming, but it has given you an excellent understanding of *exactly* what they will be looking for in the interview, and also you should now have a few basic ideas of some experiences you can use in the interview to best show your skills.

Now you have a sound understanding of the PQAs, in Part 5 we will look more closely at your life experiences to establish which ones are worth developing further. We will identify the best ones and flesh them out into fully formed top-notch pieces of evidence.

Remember, if your chosen Fire Service is using the PQA system, you can now skip the next section relating to the NFCC Leadership Framework.

PART 3 – SUMMARY

The PQAs which come up most often in interviews are:

Working with Others   Commitment to Diversity & Integrity

Commitment to Excellence   Commitment to Development

Effective Communication (score based on the way your answers to the above)

You *may* be assessed on these PQAs, which come up quite regularly:

Openness to Change   Problem Solving

Confidence & Resilience

You are *less likely* to be assessed on:

Situational Awareness - assessed during other stages of the process.

Some Key Words crop up more than once in the PQAs. Words like *Proactive, Conscientious, Enthusiastic, Empathetic, Positive, Encouraging, Adaptable...* These words should give you a pretty good clue as to the type of person they're after in the Fire Service. Basically, a decent, confident, versatile person with a bit of 'get up and go' in them. Bear these words in mind when constructing your answers later – they are very good words to include.

Some services ask questions on the Core Code of Ethics, but hopefully you will see how, by preparing for the PQAa, you are equipped to answer these questions, as "Putting Communities First", "Integrity", "Dignity and Respect", "Leadership" and "Equality, Diversity & Inclusion" align with the PQAs.

Part 4 – NFCC Leadership Framework

If you have established in Task 9 that your Fire Service is using the **NFCC Leadership Framework**, then this section is for you. Also, if your chosen Fire Service has told you they use a system of their own (probably calling it something like a "Behavioural Competency Framework") then this is the right section for you as these systems are virtually the same as the NFCC Framework. If you just couldn't find out what system they are using then this section is still good for you, as it will enable you to produce some great answers and get 100% ready for your interview.

If your chosen Fire Service is still using the **PQAs**, then ignore this section as you should have already completed Part 3 instead, so now go to Part 5.

The Leadership Framework, launched by the National Fire Chiefs' Council in 2019, is designed to replace the PQAs with 4 broad areas against which you will be measured. These areas are called "**Quadrants**". They are:

1. **PERSONAL IMPACT**
2. **OUTSTANDING LEADERSHIP**
3. **ORGANISATIONAL EFFECTIVENESS**
4. **SERVICE DELIVERY**

Each of these Quadrants can be tested at any of four levels, depending on whether you are a new applicant or an existing firefighter going for promotion. The levels are:

LEADING YOURSELF   **(New Applicants)**
LEADING OTHERS   (Supervisory Managers)
LEADING THE FUNCTION   (Middle Managers)
LEADING THE SERVICE   (Senior Officers)

If this sounds complicated, don't worry; we are about to simplify it. The Quadrants are the subject areas, and the Levels are basically what rank you're applying for – Firefighter, Watch Manager, Station Manager etc.

New applicants to the Fire Service don't need to worry about Leading Others, Leading the Function or Leading the Service.

So, we will focus solely on the initial **LEADING YOURSELF** level of each Quadrant.

The NFCC Leadership Framework can be found on the NFCC website **www.nationalfirechiefs.org.uk** (or use **www.is.gd/fireframework** to go straight to the right page). The book you're holding should give you all the information you need though.

So, for new applicants the NFCC Leadership Framework really looks like this:

New Applicants	Supervisory Managers	Middle Managers	Senior Officers
Personal Impact Level 1: Leading Yourself	Personal Impact Level 2: Leading Others	Personal Impact Level 3: Leading the Function	Personal Impact Level 4: Leading the Service
Outstanding Leadership Level 1: Leading Yourself	Outstanding Leadership Level 2: Leading Others	Outstanding Leadership Level 3: Leading the Function	Outstanding Leadership Level 4: Leading the Service
Service Delivery Level 1: Leading Yourself	Service Delivery Level 2: Leading Others	Service Delivery Level 3: Leading the Function	Service Delivery Level 4: Leading the Service
Organisational Effectiveness Level 1: Leading Yourself	Organisational Effectiveness Level 2: Leading Others	Organisational Effectiveness Level 3: Leading the Function	Organisational Effectiveness Level 4: Leading the Service

New applicants need only need to look at the left-hand column in the previous table. Many people waste precious time fretting about supervisory / middle / senior level topics which they are not going to be asked about at interview!

KEY POINT

Each of the Leadership Quadrants has four Levels, one for each level of management. As a new applicant you only need to prepare for the "Leading Yourself" level.

If you are an existing Fire Service employee going for promotion, refer to **www.is.gd/fireframework** *for the level relevant to your interview.*

So hopefully you can see that what at first looks like a complicated system, is actually fairly simple.

Next, we will look in depth at the four Quadrants at your level ("Leading Yourself") to ensure you know exactly what attributes an interviewer will be looking for in an initial recruitment interview.

Later, when we look at which qualities you've actually *got*, it should be obvious if you have any shortfalls.

Once that's done, we will move on to fixing any problems identified. Stay with the programme – there's logic and experience behind this!

Two very important things for you to understand: Firstly, when a Fire and Rescue Service conducts interviews using the Quadrants, your score is directly related to how well you can show that you hit the Quadrants.

Your interviewer will be comparing your answers against a marking sheet based on the NFCC Quadrants. Yes, there will be some room for personal judgement, but if you didn't mention anything that tallies with the Quadrant being tested, you are unlikely to score very highly for that question.

Secondly, most Fire and Rescue Services use the "experiential" or "evidence-based" format for the interview questions. These are the kind of questions that begin with *"Tell us about a time when..."* or *"Can you give an example of how you..."*

What this means is you won't get any points for saying *"I'm a great team-player."* or *"I'm fantastic at solving problems."*

You need to be able to *prove* you've got these qualities, using specific examples of real-world experiences, and whilst doing so, you need to make sure you're hitting the criteria of the Quadrant/s being tested by that question.

Yes, you can say point out that you have fantastic teamwork and problem-solving skills etc., but you need to be sure that you are backing these claims up with some concrete examples of things you have actually done, and these things need to be significant, relevant and preferably recent (ideally within the last 5 years at most).

The next task will familiarise you with the NFCC criteria – things you really need to understand in order to fully appreciate what you are aiming to prove in your interview.

TASK 11

This is a big one, and it will take a while, but it's worth it.

At the top of the next 4 pages of your workbook, write the NFCC Quadrants in the same order that they have just been introduced, so you have a sheet for each Quadrant: **Personal Impact, Outstanding Leadership, Service Delivery and Organisational Effectiveness**

Next, read through the descriptions of the Quadrants provided in the following pages. **Read them thoroughly, so you actually take them in and understand them. No skim-reading!**

Once you've read each Quadrant:

- Copy down the important information relating to each Quadrant on the corresponding page in your workbook. Include the key words and phrases and the summary;
- Describe each Quadrant, *in your own words*;
- Note down any activities, experiences or jobs you can think of that needed the qualities described by each Quadrant – just a brief heading is needed – something like *"Managing Football Team"* on your 'Service Delivery' page;
- Write down any positive personality traits under the most relevant Quadrant. If you're proud of your problem-solving skills, say, note down any examples of when you have shown this quality.

This isn't just a mindless memorisation technique; we need you to get these Quadrants firmly lodged in your mind as soon as possible – they're going to count for a great deal.

NOTE: You will never gain points for quoting Quadrants in an interview, but *knowing what they are will enable you to produce far more relevant answers*, worded in the correct style. Having the right words in your vocabulary and the right concepts in your mind will help you think and talk in the right kind of language during the interview.

This Quadrant is about the *self*.

The NFCC Framework document states: *"Personal Impact ensures we value, respect and promote equality and diversity. It's about being a positive presence on others, having personal integrity and an ability to self-manage. The focus is on self and how a manager uses leadership to create a positive, open-working environment focusing on ethics and wellbeing."*

The **Personal Impact** criteria at the "Leading Yourself" level are:

- I value inclusion and set a positive example of appropriate behaviour for peers and new starters.
- I encourage open communication and actively listen to and value others' contributions.
- I look for opportunities to learn and develop my skills and behaviours.
- I admit and learn from my mistakes and celebrate my successes with the team.
- I understand how my actions and behaviour impact on others.
- I recognise and challenge inappropriate behaviour.
- I look after myself and others, and seek help if I need it.
- I look after my mental health.

NFCC QUADRANT 1 - "PERSONAL IMPACT"

TRANSLATED INTO PLAIN ENGLISH:

Being a decent, respectful, responsible and professional member of the team and community. None of these attributes are rocket-science, but it's vitally important that you can demonstrate them.

As a Firefighter, you are expected to act in a considerate and respectful way when dealing with others, being mindful of how you are perceived. Remember that firefighters are very highly regarded by the public, so certain standards of behaviour are expected, particularly when it comes to inclusivity.

You should invite and respect ideas and opinions, never being overbearing or dismissive, but you need to be confident in confronting people where their behaviour strays beyond the bounds of decency and into intolerance.

You need to be honest with yourself and others. As Henry Ford said *"The only real mistake is the one from which we learn nothing"* so own-up to your mistakes and treat them as opportunities to develop. Your team can benefit from your mistakes, and don't forget to acknowledge their part in your successes.

Firefighters should regularly review their development needs, never be too proud or embarrassed to seek help, and be supportive of others when they need help. This may be in terms of professional development, technical skills, mentoring, emotional support, fitness or <u>mental health</u>, which is crucially important when you're dealing with traumatic incidents.

It's worth Googling *"Mind blue light programme"* for information on emergency services mental health support – it's a topical subject.

<u>KEY WORDS:</u> *RESPECTFUL, RESPECTABLE, CONSIDERATE, INCLUSIVE, EMPATHETIC, FAIR, CARING, OPEN-MINDED, RECEPTIVE, ENCOURAGING, SUPPORTIVE, APPROACHABLE, TOLERANT, UNDERSTANDING, TRUSTWORTHY*

This Quadrant is about *working with others.*

The NFCC Framework document states: *"Outstanding Leadership is about building high-performing teams and developing people to their full potential. It's about communicating with integrity, being open and honest to foster trust and building collaborative working partnership. An ambassador and role model for the Fire and Rescue Service. The focus is on others and how a manager uses leadership to create high performance teams."*

The **Outstanding Leadership** criteria at the "Leading Yourself" level are:

- I am an ambassador for the service, taking pride and responsibility for the work we do and encouraging others to do the same.
- I take responsibility and accountability for the quality of my own work.
- I value and appreciate differences in people and treat everyone with kindness and respect.
- I role model proactively, learning new skills and behaviours.

NFCC QUADRANT 2 – "OUTSTANDING LEADERSHIP"

TRANSLATED INTO PLAIN ENGLISH:

There are two main reasons why a firefighter needs leadership abilities:

Firstly, although Firefighters do not formally line-manage anyone there are many situations where you will have to take the lead, for instance when acting as casualty carer at a road traffic collision.

Secondly, the Fire Service needs good leaders, so it makes sense to recruit people with the potential to work their way up through the ranks.

Do not be alarmed though. Despite the above, it is totally acceptable for a Firefighter to have zero ambitions for promotion, and this is acknowledged in the way the NFCC have formulated this Quadrant. The focus here is on managing *yourself*. You might want to be a manager in the future; you might not. Either way managing yourself is essential.

As a firefighter you won't always have someone looking over your shoulder ensuring the quality of your work – you need to *be your own quality-control*. The Fire Service doesn't want anyone who is satisfied with low personal standards or who accepts poor work from colleagues.

You will be trusted to get on with the job, professionally and diligently and you will be expected to address shortfalls in others in a tactful and constructive way, in the interests of effective team working.

Firefighters are role models, and must respect diversity in all its forms, treating people with due consideration. Remaining open to new perspectives and receptive to new ways of working are key to continuous development.

NOTE: Some Fire Services call this Quadrant **"Working Together"**.

<u>**KEY WORDS:**</u> *CONSCIENTIOUS, OPEN, DILLIGENT, METICULOUS, CONSIDERATE, CONSISTENT, POSITIVE ROLE-MODEL, HIGH STANDARDS, EFFICIENT, THOROUGH, RELIABLE, TEAM-PLAYER.*

This Quadrant is *task-orientated*.

The NFCC Framework document states: *"Service Delivery is about delivering high quality services now and into the future. It's about intelligent problem solving with an outcome focussed approach, continuous improvement and value for money to our customers. The focus is on task and how a manager uses leadership to produce outcome-focussed results which meet customer needs."*

The **Service Delivery** criteria at the "Leading Yourself" level are:

- I am focussed on customer needs in my approach to my work, including issues of safeguarding and inclusion.
- I act as a role model for my community.
- I plan ahead and prioritise my work, managing my time effectively to get things done.
- I am careful with all types of resources (money, time, materials, fuel and energy) to provide value for money.
- I spot opportunities to improve the way we do things for people, and put ideas forward.
- I actively contribute to problem-solving and take time to understand the issues fully.
- I take decisions based on supporting evidence, risk, and my prior knowledge of good practice.
- I work to foster trust with others and build constructive working relationships to achieve goals.
- I find out about my local community and risks, to ensure we are offering the best service.

NFCC QUADRANT 3 – "SERVICE DELIVERY"

TRANSLATED INTO PLAIN ENGLISH:

In the past, the Fire Service would arrive, drench your house with water, and leave. Nowadays at a property fire we are expected to be far more aware of other needs such as salvaging and securing property afterwards, and helping to ensure temporary accommodation whilst being alert to, and addressing other issues such as domestic abuse, hoarding and radicalisation.

Notice the word "customer". This signifies a shift in approach from a quasi-military agency dealing solely with incidents and casualties to more of an all-round service, focused on providing the best value for money to the communities who pay our wages.

Key to providing an efficient and effective service to our communities is making a concerted effort to reflect on the way we work and pushing for improvements. Could you be doing home safety checks in a better way, for instance? If the evidence in your area shows that elderly people are suffering disproportionately from house fires, it may be worth developing a relationship with the local authority's Home Care department to you ensure you are able to target the most vulnerable people first.

Prioritising activities in an evidence-based way is likely to achieve much more of a reduction in risk per-pound than just randomly visiting houses near the fire station. Your Fire Service is likely to have a team of people on hand who are able to help with this kind of initiative. Remember, when dealing with other agencies and the public, you are an ambassador for the Fire Service, and high standards are essential. You need to continually assess your work and the work going on around you, to see if there is a better, more cost-effective way of producing the same or better results. The idea is to *"do more for less"*.

KEY WORDS: *ANALYTICAL, PROBLEM-SOLVING, PLANNING, SAFEGUARDING, ROLE-MODEL, EFFICIENT, CUSTOMER-FOCUSED, INCLUSIVE, TIME-MANAGEMENT, PROACTIVE, EVIDENCE-BASED.*

This Quadrant is about the *organisation*.

The NFCC Framework document states: *"Organisational Effectiveness is ensuring everything we do is linked to organisational plans and values. It's driving the mission and ensuring decisions and actions are beneficial to the customer. The focus is on the organisation and how a manager uses leadership to continuously improve, innovate and change."*

The **Organisational Effectiveness** criteria at the "Leading Yourself" level are:

- I know what the key organisational goals are and how I make a difference.
- I work within the organisations policies, procedures and processes.
- I speak out promptly if I see or hear of a safety or organisational risk.
- I offer ideas and feedback to improve our services, and take on board other's ideas.
- I continuously seek to improve my performance to contribute to organisational goals.
- I am open to, and positively engage with, new ways of working.
- I positively seek organisational information about how well we are doing and what is changing.
- I can be trusted with sensitive information.

NFCC QUADRANT 4 – "ORGANISATIONAL EFFECTIVENESS"

TRANSLATED INTO PLAIN ENGLISH:

It's all well and good working hard and doing what *seems right*, but you need to be sure that what you are doing is in line with the goals and mission of the organisation, otherwise you will have trouble demonstrating that all your hard work was worthwhile.

This quadrant is about working *smarter*. Your chosen Fire Service's website should tell you what their organisational values are, and may include some kind of plan or priorities for the next few years. These may be specific targets like reducing deliberate fires to a certain number, or more general goals like reducing the carbon footprint. The important thing is that you appreciate the need to directly link every piece of work you do in the Fire Service to one or more of the organisation's goals.

You may identify a need to develop yourself personally to acquire certain skills that help the organisation reach its goals. For instance, you might enrol on a course to help with presentation skills so you can deliver more effective fire safety talks to community groups, which aligns with the organisation's goals to engage with the community and reduce fires in the home.

Your Fire Service will have set procedures for most activities, and it is important that you are aware of the importance of working within these parameters and the steps to take if you see any breaches, for instance reporting the accidental release of personal information. Where you notice a potential efficiency or safety gain, you need to feed these ideas back to the relevant people to enable continuous improvement.

KEY WORDS: FOCUSED, UP TO DATE, PROACTVE, OPEN TO CHANGE, INNOVATIVE, TRUSTWORTHY, CONSCIENTIOUS, WELL-INFORMED.

KEY POINT

A few Fire Services have taken the NFCC Framework and added their own content to the four official Quadrants, so you may find an additional section, often involving *"Health, Safety and Wellbeing"*. If this is the case, pay very close attention to the extra criteria as it's obviously something that your chosen Fire Service considers important enough to have its own category.

When a Fire Service adopts and adapts the NFCC Framework like this they will usually give it name like "Behavioural Competency Framework". Don't be thrown by this – it's still the NFCC Framework, just with an extra bit bolted-on.

Some Fire and Rescue Services ask questions on the Core Code of Ethics, but hopefully you will see how, by preparing for the NFCC Quadrants, you are equipped to answer these questions, as "Putting Communities First", "Integrity", "Dignity and Respect", "Leadership" and "Equality, Diversity & Inclusion" align with the Quadrants.

So, that's all the NFCC Quadrants. Go back to the Task 11 workbox and ensure you have completed it fully. For each Quadrant you should now have a summary with key words and phrases, a description of it in your own words, a list of examples where you demonstrated the qualities described, and any key attributes that you may have which tally with the Quadrants.

This task may have been difficult and time-consuming, but it has given you an excellent understanding of *exactly* what they will be looking for in the interview, and also you should now have a few basic ideas of some experiences you can use in the interview to best show your skills.

Now you have a sound understanding of the Quadrants, in Part 5 we will look more closely at your life experiences to establish which ones are worth developing further. We will identify the best ones and flesh them out into fully formed top-notch pieces of evidence.

The NFCC Quadrants are:

1. **PERSONAL IMPACT**
2. **OUTSTANDING LEADERSHIP**
3. **ORGANISATIONAL EFFECTIVENESS**
4. **SERVICE DELIVERY**

These Quadrants can be tested at different levels depending on your rank. As a new applicant you only need to concern yourself with the first level, which is called "Leading Yourself". To avoid confusion, that's the only level we discuss in this book.

You may notice some Key Words crop up more than once in the Quadrants. Words like *Proactive, Role-Model, Trustworthy...* These words should give you a pretty good clue as to the type of person they're after in the Fire Service. Basically, a decent, confident, versatile person with a bit of 'get up and go' in them. Bear these words in mind when constructing your answers later – they are very good words to include.

Part 5 – Selecting and Writing Your Best Examples

Icebreaker Answers

Some interviewers like to ask you a casual question at the start, which is not part of the official interview and is not marked. This is supposed to "put you at ease" (like that's going to work!) Often the question will be the dreaded *"Tell me a bit about yourself"* or a slightly more relevant *"Why do you want to join the Fire and Rescue Service?"* Even though these questions are not officially marked, your response is vitally important, since the interviewer is likely to be subconsciously making judgements about you already (and probably started doing so the moment you walked through the door). They may ask you to outline what you already know about the Fire Service, which is a great opportunity to show them that you're so keen and proactive that you've done some research in your own time. The answer you prepared in Part 2 will stand you in very good stead for this kind of question.

If you are not expecting it, this icebreaker question can really throw you off your stride. This is excellent news for you though, because the people you are competing against probably do not have the advantage of your pre-prepared answers. This kind of icebreaker question plays right into your hands.

Even if this question is non-Fire Service-related, such as *tell us a bit about yourself*, then it is important that everything you say is nudging the interviewer towards seeing you as Fire Service material. However, remember that as this is just an icebreaker, you shouldn't ramble on for too long. A minute is enough to tell them a bit about your current position, hobbies (very briefly), proudest achievements, goals and fitness regime. Be enthusiastic. Bring it to a close by mentioning that you really want to join the Fire Service because of the reasons you wrote down in Part 1 and that you think you will be a great Firefighter because of your self-discipline/love of teamwork/fitness/ability to learn new skills.

If the icebreaker question is somehow related to the Fire Service, then this is your chance to crowbar in all the facts that you picked up during your research in Part 2. You need to prepare an answer that showcases your knowledge, but you need to vary your tone otherwise you'll sound like a robot reciting a list.

A perfect answer to a <u>Non-Fire Service-Related Icebreaker Question</u> such as *"Tell me a bit about yourself"* would be something like this (or a shorter version, depending on the pace of the interview):

"I'm Andy Smith, from Knapforth, married with two kids, I enjoy 5-a-side and cycling. I have been working in automotive engineering for eight years, in Ford for the last six. I'm currently a supervisor of a team of ten staff in an engine plant – the people in my team come from all kinds of backgrounds and a wide age range so I've learned a lot about teamwork and how to use different techniques to motivate people to get work done.

The work we do has to be performed to a very high standard and mistakes are expensive, so it's really important that each member of the team completes their job with precision and attention to detail or else things go wrong and then we end up missing targets and costing the company money. When I was doing the manufacturing side of things myself, I always prided myself on high standards and now I'm supervising I expect my team to turn out top-quality work too.

I love teamwork and I think I'm good at motivating people, whether in sport or in work. The team was underperforming when I took over and it was a great challenge to get things back on track; I've found it very rewarding to turn things around – we're now one of the best teams in the company in terms of productivity. I focused the team on the work by explaining the consequences of every small task, and this has motivated them to do well. Also, whereas my predecessor was very strict and wouldn't tolerate errors, leading to people concealing mistakes which led to bigger problems down the line, I like to think I have created an atmosphere where my team members can approach me with their concerns and admit mistakes so we can nip things in the bud, learn and move on.

I think communication is vitally important in a team situation and this is central to the way I work. I have implemented regular informal meetings where we can all raise issues, and I've reinstated formal appraisals, which had previously gone by the wayside.

One of my proudest achievements was introducing free weekly English lessons for our staff. I made a business case to the company to pay for this by showing how the language barrier was affecting efficiency and morale within the team, which has several Eastern Europeans. As well as helping the team perform better, a positive side-effect of this was better relations within the team as they can now socialise better.

It's because I'm motivated, good at teamwork and good at communicating and problem solving that I think I would fit right in and hit the ground running as a Firefighter, and hopefully eventually move up the ranks through hard work. I enjoy my job, but I've wanted to be a Firefighter since I was young and would like to feel like my skills hard work are helping people. I enjoyed solving problems in a fast-paced environment back when I was in the Army and would love to get back to that kind of challenge."

It's worth checking out *"How to answer interview icebreaker questions"* on YouTube at this point – there are some good pointers on there. The above is just fine though if you are pushed for time.

Don't worry if the above answer seems a little over-the-top or a lot to remember – this example is the *ideal* answer that you would give if you had a perfect memory or were reading it from your notes with loads of time available.

A perfect answer to a <u>Fire Service-Related Icebreaker Question</u> such as *"Tell me what you know about Hamptonshire Fire and Rescue Service"* would be something like this:

"Hamptonshire Fire and Rescue Service was formed in 1994 when Westampton and Middleshire Fire Brigades joined together, making it the sixth biggest Fire Service in the country, serving a population of around three million people.

The Chief Fire Officer is Gordon Brazier and there are 34 fire stations in total; 20 of them are Retained stations and the remaining 14 are Wholetime. The area you cover includes cities, coastline and rural communities.

I know the aim of WFRS is to make Westhampton the safest place to live, work and travel and your mission is to protect and save – to prevent emergencies, create safer communities and respond to save life. I can see that you are currently running a campaign to teach schoolchildren about the dangers of grassfires, called 'Flames Aren't Games' and I know you have previously run awareness campaigns about road safety and chip-pan fires, so you're obviously committed to the preventative side of things which I am all in favour of.

Actually, I have a particular interest in the co-responding work you are doing with the Ambulance Service because I have experience of dealing with trauma patients from my time in the Army, and would like to get involved with that – I think I may have some positive ideas. From speaking to the crews at Westhampton Central Station I know there's a bit of conflict regarding co-responding with the ambulance service and the union has raised objections. They also mentioned that one of the main challenges they face at the moment is combatting deliberate fires, especially in rural areas, and I know you're working with the police and youth groups to try and tackle the problem. That's something I'd be really keen to get involved with.

Like most Fire and Rescue Services you're having to do this and all your other work despite budget cuts and the loss of three stations over the past two years. It must take some clever planning to accomplish all this whilst maintaining staff morale. We've faced similar challenges in my workplace, so I'm used to finding ways to do more for less. Your recent review shows that you face challenges with culture issues and it's reassuring how seriously you are taking this – the positive steps you're taking show a commitment to creating an inclusive workplace."

To give you an idea of pace, the above answer should take around ninety seconds to two minutes read out at a conversational speed, with the usual number of *umms* and *errs* thrown in.

Don't be alarmed if you think the above answer seems unachievable, complex and detailed. Don't worry if you're thinking *"Oh my god, that's just not the way I speak, I'll never be able to rattle all that lot off in an interview"*. This is a *perfect* answer. It would be very impressive indeed if you could reel off such a comprehensive collection of facts and even more impressive if you could do so in a relaxed and human-sounding way but that's not what we're actually trying to achieve here.

The idea is, just *try* to memorise *all* the detail, so that in the interview, even if you only remember *half* of it and get it out in your normal conversational way of speaking, you will be head and shoulders above most other people that you are competing against, who haven't tried to memorise *any* of it and are making it up as they go along, and floundering in the process. Since your competition will be making up their answers on the spot, they'll be using all their brainpower to *think of new stuff* whereas you'll just be trying to remember *things you already know*, which is much easier.

Just a word of warning though, be careful how much technical information you include about stations, pumps and special appliances etc. as you could easily come across as a "spotter" – slang for a Fire Service nerd and social misfit who is obsessed with the Fire Service and unlikely to fit in with the normal people on the watch. Basically, go easy on the technical detail.

TASK 12

Prepare two icebreaker answers based on the examples above:

A generic and non-Fire Service-related example with a link to your suitability at the end.

A Fire Service-specific example including all the facts you have learned about the Fire Service you are applying for. Include a link to how you are ideally suited to working with them at the end.

Each example needs to be between 1 and 2 minutes in length when read out loud at normal speed.

Remember that these examples are your "Gold Standard", perfect answers, and that you should try to memorise as much of them as possible, so during the interview itself, you'll have a ready-made bank of material to reach for.

You will be doing exceptionally well if you only manage to remember half of it. You will probably find that the material is queuing up in your brain as you're speaking – this is a very good thing. Things may come out in a different order, which is fine.

Remembering scraps of pre-prepared material is far easier than thinking up new stuff on the spot.

Remember: Train Hard, Fight Easy!

Selecting your Best Examples – The Matrix

In this section we are going to use a simple and highly effective method to compare your experiences against the criteria your interviewer will be marking you against, to see which experiences are worth polishing-up into the ones you are going to use in the interview.

Don't worry if this bit seems a little fiddly or complex. You only have to do it once, and you don't have to worry about it in the interview. We are just filtering your life experiences to identify your most valuable ones.

Your life experiences are your **EVIDENCE** you will be using to prove you have the right qualities to be a firefighter. This is the *"proper preparation"* we mentioned in the introduction.

You've probably got a lot of different things you could talk about in an interview, but we want to work out which ones are the killer pieces of evidence that will carry you through. It's not enough to just think about what you've done in your life and talk about the things that you *think* are the best. You need to sit down and do it in a calculated way, to make sure you're focusing on your strengths to really sell yourself and maximise your chances of success.

Also, you don't want to have to remember any more than **six** pieces of evidence as this is simply too difficult given the amount of detail you need to include in each one. The ideal number is probably five as this gives you some freedom to choose. You may be able to rely on just four examples if they are good all-rounders, with each one hitting multiple PQAs/NFCC criteria.

The method we are going to use will help you discard the mediocre answers you might have given and move forward with just the real belters. Ideally your evidence should be drawn from different experiences as you don't want the interviewer to feel like they are being told the same story multiple times from different angles. However, it's ok to use examples based on the same job/event as long as the situation being described, and the actions you took are significantly different in each case.

TASK 13

On a fresh page in your workbook, down the left-hand side, list all the experiences that you came up with in Task 10 or 11 whilst going through the PQAs/Quadrants – sum each one up with a title. Add any new experiences you can think of that you might like to refer to in the interview. These experiences can be projects you completed in work, events you organised, responsibilities you have taken on for local sports clubs or your workplace, charity events you have been involved with, that kind of thing – anything that helps you to show you are a decent, positive, enthusiastic team worker with good communications skills.

Next, across the top of the page, write the names of the 9 PQAs or 4 Quadrants (whichever your Fire Service is using). Now get a ruler and divide the page up into a table. There is an example on the next page showing what it should look like for a candidate applying for a job with a Fire Service which is using the PQA system. If your Fire Service is using the Quadrants it won't have as many columns.

This next bit is vitally important so take a bit of time to do it properly. You need to assess each piece of evidence and mark it from 0 to 3 depending on how well it matches the PQA or Quadrant.

Our example candidate coached Under 16's football and judged that piece of evidence as a 3 for *Excellence*, *Development* and *Working with Others* because they supported and mentored people and improved the way the club was run by making positive changes. Perhaps that piece of evidence only warrants a "0" for *Situational Awareness* though. Do this for every piece of evidence.

Finally, on the right, tot-up the scores to see which pieces of evidence are the best "all-rounders".

EXAMPLE	WORKING WITH OTHERS	COMMITMENT TO DIVERSITY & INTEGRITY	COMMITMENT TO EXCELLENCE	COMMITMENT TO DEVELOPMENT	EFFECTIVE COMMUNICATION	OPENNESS TO CHANGE	PROBLEM SOLVING	CONFIDENCE AND RESILIENCE	SITUATIONAL AWARENESS	TOTALS
Coaching Under 16s	3	2	3	3	2	1	1	2	0	17
House Renovation	1	0	1	2	1	2	3	3	3	16
Stewarding in Stadium	3	1	1	0	2	1	0	2	2	12
Implementing New Production Process	1	0	3	2	1	2	3	1	0	13
Confronting Colleague About Racism	2	3	1	1	2	1	0	3	0	13
Volunteering to Lead Community Scheme	3	3	3	2	1	2	0	2	0	16
~~Developing Own Fitness Programme~~	0	0	3	3	0	1	1	1	0	9
New Safety Equipment Idea	1	0	3	1	1	3	3	1	0	13
Charity Shop Disabled Changing Problem	3	3	2	1	3	3	3	1	1	20
~~Organising Charity 10k~~	2	0	1	0	2	0	1	1	0	7
Warehouse Re-Org	1	0	3	2	1	2	3	1	0	13
Fundraising for Ellie's Treatment	3	1	2	0	2	1	3	3	0	16

You should end up with a table looking like this (for PQA candidates). There are blank versions for both PQA and Quadrant systems at the end of this book for you to use. The PQA/Quadrant Matrix is a good visual representation of your evidence, showing which ones are the strongest, and so worth developing.

You can pretty much discard your worst examples at this point as they will not help your cause. In the example above, the person completing the matrix has crossed out the worst two examples as it is clear they are not worth pursuing.

The best thing about this method is that it doesn't rely on gut-feeling. By using the PQAs and Quadrants as the marking scheme, you are grading your evidence using *the same criteria* that your interviewer will be using.

Some of the results may surprise you. Something which you thought might have been great, like organising a charity fun-run, might actually turn out to be fairly useless as a piece of evidence in its own right as it was a bit one-dimensional, although you may be able to mention it briefly as part of another piece of evidence.

Conversely, something seemingly simple, such as the time you noticed a wheelchair-user struggling in the charity shop you were volunteering in, so you sorted out proper changing facilities; that piece of evidence may pop out as unexpectedly useful and you might find yourself developing it further.

If you have lots of pieces of evidence with the same score, a good way of working out which one is the most useful is to look at them and see whether any individual piece of evidence is the *only one* to hit certain criteria. In the example above, there are three pieces of evidence worth 16 points, but only one of those (*House Renovation*) could be used to demonstrate the *Situational Awareness* PQA, so it is probably worth choosing that one over the others.

Similarly, only one piece of evidence scores 3 for *Effective Communication*, so that piece of evidence (*Disabled Charity Shop Changing*) would need to be prioritised even if it wasn't already the highest score overall.

At this point you may hear alarm bells ringing if you have a column with nothing in it – a PQA or Quadrant that you just can't seem to hit. If you're working with PQAs, remember that the ones on the right are less likely to be tested in an interview than the ones on the left. All is not lost if you've got currently got nothing for Situational Awareness, but have a real good think and re-read that PQA to try and jog your memory.

Any PQAs missing in the left columns though, you need to take action, and depending on when your interview is, it may not be too late.

Candidates using the NFCC Framework column don't need to worry about which criteria are most often tested, as they're all used.

I know someone who, with a couple of months to go, realised that he was going to find it very hard to show any kind of *Commitment to Diversity and Integrity* using his set of life experiences. He was not the kind to leave anything to chance though and because he had completed the matrix exercise, he had done the analysis and identified this shortfall in good time.

To address the problem, he volunteered to work a couple of shifts a week a charity shop. It wasn't even particularly onerous, literally just a couple of mornings when he was off work, mostly spent chatting with the friendly customers – he actually enjoyed it. Whilst he was there, he got involved with a small project that showed he had some good qualities.

What this meant was, by the time his interview came, he had managed to gain a perfect piece of experience which met this and several other criteria – in fact this is the example mentioned previously; it's the one involving a disabled changing room. We will use this piece of evidence as an example in the next section to show how to write up your evidence in the best format.

What this person did was effectively to manufacture a genuine life experience specifically to demonstrate that he had the right attributes to be a firefighter. This may sound extremely calculated but really, he just took a good look at his strengths and weaknesses and took appropriate steps to make himself a more rounded candidate to get the job he really wanted.

Note that the above example applies equally to PQA and Quadrant candidates.

PART 5 – SUMMARY

There are two main types of questions in the interview.

The first type is the *Icebreaker,* which isn't usually marked. Don't underestimate the importance of the icebreaker – the interview panel will be paying very close attention to what you say and how you say it. It's your first opportunity to really sell yourself and subconscious judgements are made at this point.

Most people are flummoxed and waste the opportunity that the icebreaker gives you, but you now have two fantastic answers ready to wheel-in. You can use this opportunity to show how well you prepare, how well you will fit in, how keen you are and what skills you can bring.

The second type of question is the more formal competency-based question which aims to probe your skills and experience. Usually, these questions are marked using the PQAs and Quadrants as scoring criteria. Most people just tell whichever story they think will fit the question at the time and often end up rambling about something fairly irrelevant. Instead of relying on gut-feeling and improvisation though, you should now have scientifically whittled down your experience to the most valuable pieces of evidence, which will suit any question they can ask you.

Next, we need to take these examples of life experiences and turn them into top quality Fire Service interview answers.

In addition, we need to make sure you can identify the key words and phrases lurking in the questions that will tell you which PQA or Quadrant is being tested. You need to be able to select the right one of your final four or five pieces of evidence to match the question being asked. There's no point doing all this work perfecting your answers if you provide you perfect *Personal Impact* answer to a question designed to test your *Outstanding Leadership.* We will ensure you have the tools to avoid this trap later.

Part 6 – Fine-Tuning Your Answers

The B.A.C.O.N. Method

During the interview, candidates are typically expected to answer each question within around five minutes, sometimes ten. This timing information is usually included in the information pack you get sent prior to the recruitment process, if not, call the HR department – they should tell you over the phone.

All of the examples and timings in this section are based on 5-minute answers. If your chosen Fire Service is allocating 10 minutes per answer, then simply double every number quoted below. Don't go into an interview with 5-minute answers when you've got 10 minutes available. You need to make every second count. The timings below are guidelines – don't think the Actions section needs to be *exactly* two/four minutes; they're just there to show you the relative importance of each section.

Probably the most tried and tested method for answering competency-based (*"Tell us about a time when you..."*) questions is the **S.T.A.R.** method in which you describe a **S**ituation you were in, the **T**ask which needed completing, the **A**ctions you took and what the end **R**esults were. This technique is great because it is quite straightforward and produces a natural-sounding response. It is also stops you from jumping ahead and skipping the important bits, and it tends to keep you calm and composed in the interview as you don't have to do any thinking on the fly once you've set-off on a pre-scripted answer.

Lots of people will be using the S.T.A.R. method. You can too if you wish. There is nothing really wrong with it and there is plenty of information about it available online if you want to keep things simple.

However, you may find that, when using the S.T.A.R. method, the interviewer will keep prompting you for more information. Also, you want to stand out in the interview and be better than the rest. So, we will be using a more Fire Service-friendly system which builds on the best bits of the S.T.A.R. method and aligns it with the demands of a Fire Service PQA or NFCC Framework-based interview. This method is based on my personal experience from interviewing hundreds of candidates over many years. It is also the method I have used myself every time I have passed an interview in the Fire Service. The acronym isn't as glamorous sounding as S.T.A.R., but it's no less memorable:

B.A.C.O.N.

(Apologies to vegetarians and member of the Islamic / Jewish communities)

How does it work though?

Well, beginning with **Background**, which includes both the situation you were in *and* your own personal feelings about it, you then move onto describing your **Actions**, firstly in broad terms and then focusing tightly on one particular element of what you did. Next you will mention any **Challenges** or obstacles and how you overcame them before explaining the **Outcomes** in relation to the specific problem and also any wider implications. Finally, in the **Now What**? Section you will reflect on what you learned from the experience and how you have used/can use it to improve things for you and others in future.

KEY POINT

When you're writing out your draft interview answers, remember that examples featuring phrases like

"I noticed / I decided / I realised / I took it upon myself / I wanted to..."

are always **way** more impressive than

"We were told / my manager asked us to / We had to / We needed to".

You need to emphasise the fact that **you** did whatever **you** did off **your** own bat, using **your** own initiative, not just because it was the procedure or someone told you or your team to do it, or it just had to be done.

You need to be using the word *"I"* a lot more than the word *"we"*. Yes, the Fire Service is all about teamwork, but the interview is all about **you**.

The start of your answer is all about setting the scene. You need to provide an overview with enough context and background so that the rest of the story makes sense. Include details of **where** you were, **what** you were doing, **when** it was, and **who** you were working with.

You should also explain **why** you were doing it, as this tells the interviewers what your drivers are. Don't just say *"I had to change x because it's part of my job"*. You need to state your personal motivations. *"I wanted to change x because I take pride in my work and could see an opportunity for improvement to make things safer/more efficient"* tells the interviewer a lot more about the kind of person you are. The Background section gives you an opportunity to introduce glimpses of *your* background as well as the background of the situation you were in.

It is likely that you will be describing a situation that your interviewers are not familiar with – something specific to your place of work. Because of this is it is **vitally** important that you explain any jargon or acronyms – if you forget this, you will drop points for Communications.

I like to be kind to interviewees, so I'll ask the candidates *"Stop there a minute – can you please just explain what the ABC Team / XYZ Unit / FFS Machine is?"* but I know several less forgiving interviewers who just let the candidate ramble on whilst deducting points for not clarifying these things.

This part of your answer should take less than a minute but don't race through it. It may feel like you're wasting valuable time waffling about the situation, but it's actually a great opportunity to find your voice and begin to sell your positives. Set a steady pace; take your time.

Let's look at an example of how to write a good Background using the example we mentioned before, involving the person who made changes to a charity shop to make it more accessible to people with disabilities. If you look back at the matrix, you will see that this example hits 5 different PQAs, so we need to bear those qualities in mind when writing it up. Importantly, it is the only example on the highlighted shortlist that hits *Openness to*

Change PQA, so we need to make extra sure our final answer hits all of the criteria detailed in that PQA. Here we go:

I volunteer twice weekly in my local BHF charity shop. That's the British Heart Foundation by the way. I like to do my bit for my community and it's good to feel like I'm giving something back.

I've been there for around six months, and I'm trusted with running the place whenever I'm there. I'm always on the lookout for ways to improve things, and I've been able to make a few changes.

For example, a few months back I was working on my own when I noticed that a lady in wheelchair couldn't access the small changing room at the back of the shop and was clearly finding it frustrating. At the time all I could do was apologise and let her use the storeroom instead, which wasn't ideal.

I wasn't satisfied with this though, and I felt the urge to make the shop more accessible to people who use wheelchairs. It was the decent thing to do on a personal level and also, we as an organisation need to be as inclusive as possible. It was also a bit of challenge to solve, and besides, the Disability Discrimination Act and the Equality Act say you should make reasonable adjustments to allow disabled access.

The above example paints a good enough picture of the situation. More importantly, it also plants in the interviewer's mind valuable positive information about your values, personality, motivations and knowledge.

Already you can see why this structure is going to be better than S.T.A.R. – rather than wasting the first 20% of your answer describing a situation (and not scoring any points), here you're using the time to show the interviewer that you are a trustworthy, considerate, proactive, improvement-seeking problem solver who is aware of Equality and Diversity issues!

You can really maximise the opportunity to sell yourself in the Background section by dropping in a few nuggets about *your own background*, as above.

This section is the meat of your bacon sandwich and will probably score you the majority of your points, so you need to make every word count here.

You should have described already how you became aware of the situation in the Background section. Here you will be talking about how *you* dealt with it, and you need to describe your actions in a logical and easy to follow way.

First, you should talk about how you analysed the situation, then how you considered several solutions, how you worked out which was the best one, and then how you came up with a plan to get the solution implemented.

It's also good to talk about how you divided your plan up into manageable chunks and set timescales and milestones to ensure you hit your target deadline. Something like *"I made it my goal to get 'Task X' completed by the end of the week and 'Task Y' completed by the end of November so we could get the whole thing finished by the Christmas break"*.

You should be specific about how you communicated the plan to the people involved (email/face-to-face/group meetings etc.) and how you motivated people. For example, you could mention that you sold the idea to your colleagues in terms of *"Look, if we put in this extra work in the short term, it will make the system better so our jobs will be easier in the long term"*.

You will also need to emphasise that *you* drove the project through to completion, monitoring progress along the way against the milestones and timescales you set.

You need to be specific about what you were aiming for and how you planned to measure the eventual success. Whilst doing all of this, it is important not to reply entirely on general actions with woolly phrases like *"I organised x, I arranged y"*; you need to focus-in on some specific tasks, to show your personal involvement. Phrases like *"I rang the area manager and arranged a meeting to see what could be done"* or *"I took Jeff to one side and explained exactly what I needed him to do"* fit the bill here.

If this all sounds like too much to cram in, or perhaps it might sound like a load of corporate business-babble if you've never done this kind of thing before, but it's really just a checklist of things to include to show an interviewer that you're methodical in the way you work.

These nuggets all tell the interviewer that you don't just go full pelt at a problem without really thinking it through.

Carrying on with the charity shop example, let's look at how to construct a good Actions section.

Once I'd set my mind to fixing this problem, I spoke to the manager to see if there was a budget for getting something in place but unfortunately there was no money available, so I had to be resourceful and come up with some cost-neutral ideas.

Some of the ideas I came up with included tidying up a corner of the storeroom at the rear of the shop and making that into a changing room, but that wasn't ideal as the storeroom is also the fire escape.

I also asked the neighbouring charity shop if we could share their changing room, which we did, temporarily, but it meant customers taking clothing out of our shop, often in the rain, which wasn't ideal either.

In the end I was inspired by the TV programme "DIY SOS", and I appealed on social media for a local builder to come and construct a stud-wall changing room free of charge. In exchange I said they could fix a poster to the wall saying "Changing room kindly donated by Such-and-Such Construction" so they would get some publicity in return for their efforts.

I've never been involved in anything like this before, so I enlisted the help of the customer who had originally needed the disabled changing room, and she was happy to advise on the dimensions required.

As a result of the social media post some local tradesmen and a local builders' merchant got in touch and offered materials and labour for free. I arranged for the tradesmen to meet me at the shop after closing one evening and explained exactly what was required, showing them the design I'd sketched. Once the carpenter, plasterer and electrician had told me what materials they needed I was able to arrange suitable times for them to return and carry out the work. I coordinated the order with the builders' merchant and made sure everything was delivered in time for the work to begin.

I scheduled the work to take place over three evenings and I planned to tape off the area involved to minimise disruption and keep customers safe. I explained to the tradespeople the importance of keeping to the agreed dates so we could get the shop back in order as soon as possible.

I rang them all a couple of times in the days leading up to their slots, just as a polite reminder to help make sure they turned up as agreed.

Once I had organised everything, I got in touch with the local free newspaper to see if they would be interested in doing a small piece about this project, as it would be good publicity for the charity and also for the people doing the work. They agreed to send a photographer around when the work was finished, so I arranged a date for everyone involve to come back for photographs.

If the question is project-related, then the following bullet-points will help you construct a good Actions section. You don't need to use these if the question relates to "soft-skills" testing your interpersonal qualities

- Analysed the problem & identified possible solutions
- Evaluated them all (Strengths/Weaknesses/Opportunities/Threats)
- Selected the best option; explain *why* it's the best
- Formulated a plan & subdivided it if it's complex
- Established milestones and timescales (specific and measurable)
- Clearly established what success looks like
- Communicated your plan to all involved
- Continually evaluated progress against expected outcomes
- Explained specific low-level tasks
- Ensured you properly expressed the level of difficulty of the task

The Challenges section is your chance to describe what obstacles you had to overcome to deal with the situation effectively. If there were no challenges, then perhaps the task you are describing is too basic – there must have been *something* that made it difficult, otherwise you're probably just discussing an everyday, unremarkable piece of work.

Challenges can be external factors (other people's actions or resistance, unexpected expense, unforeseen circumstances etc.) or internal to you (your own fears, lack of training, subject knowledge etc.)

This is also a good place to talk about any mistakes you made and how you dealt with them. Do not be afraid to talk about your mistakes in an interview. Being honest about your mistakes shows you have a professional and mature attitude. Nobody is perfect, but people who conceal or can't see their mistakes are much less effective in the workplace. Just be sure to explain how you *identified* your mistake, how you *owned-up to* it, how you *took responsibility* for rectifying it and how you *took steps to avoid repeating the mistake.* Learning from your mistakes is a very good thing.

In the example we're using, the Challenges section might be as follows:

When the carpenter was halfway through the job, he raised concerns about the dimensions. He said he'd just completed another job involving disabled access and the measurements given by the wheelchair user were wrong.

I told him to continue using the measurements I had been given as I was sure that a person who uses a wheelchair every day would know what they were talking about. I wasn't 100% sure though, so whilst he was working, I downloaded and printed off the official disabled access guide used in construction.

The guide specified exactly how big a changing room should be, with doorway widths etc. It turns out that the carpenter was right, and the wheelchair-user had given incorrect dimensions, so I let him know straight away before he did any more work.

Thankfully I stopped him early enough so that it wasn't a major issue, and he was able to adjust things no problem. When I reflected on this afterwards, I realised I'd put too much importance on the word of one person who I had assumed was knowledgeable in the subject, without double-checking.

It's taught me that you really need to verify your information whenever possible when formulating a plan, and get the official version if possible.

As you can see, the Challenges section doesn't need to be huge, just big enough to outline something that caused you some extra level of difficulty that meant you had to adapt, overcome or deal with a mistake. You should be able to cover this in a minute.

The above example is all about a mistake, but it could equally be an example of an unforeseen problem like someone not turning up on time, a machine breaking, someone going off on the sick mid-project, being asked to change direction in the middle of a piece of work, or even just having to do a job whilst juggling numerous other tasks.

Usually, people totally squander the opportunity presented by the Result section of a S.T.A.R. answer, by saying words to the effect of *"...and it all went to plan, and we achieved everything we set out to do, on time and on budget."*

Ok, that's a great result in the real world, but it it's not actually very interesting and it suggests that you did a load of work for a pretty insignificant end result. You need to emphasise the positive impact of your work and give your interviewer something to write down and read through later on when collating your marks.

The Outcome section of your answer should, of course, confirm the end result of the piece of work being described (hopefully a positive one, but if not, you need to show that you learned/rectified for the future etc.), but you need to do so in detail. You need to explain how you evaluated the end result and how you assessed the immediate and wider consequences.

Your outcomes need to be measurable, and you need to be able to show how you checked you'd achieved what you set out to do.

Using a hypothetical example, something like *"after I arranged for the extra staff to join our team, the factory seemed to run a lot better, and everyone seemed happier"* is too vague.

To be more convincing, you need to be more specific, so something like *"after I arranged for the extra staff, our productivity went up by 25% within two months and the staff satisfaction survey showed a 70% increase in people saying they were Satisfied or Very Satisfied with their job due to the more manageable workloads."*

Carrying on with the charity shop example, a good Outcome would be something like this:

Following a few more hiccups, including me having to find a replacement painter and decorator at short notice as the first one let us down, the changing room was completed over three evenings as planned. I checked the dimensions against the guide, and it was exactly right.

As I mentioned, I had contacted the local free newspaper and invited them to come and do a piece on what we'd done, and I made sure that all the tradespeople who'd helped out were present for the photos.

The article was featured on the local news website as well as in the newspaper and I made sure it received exposure on the local social media sites and the charity's Facebook page.

It ended up being a real good-news story and a great bit of publicity for the tradespeople as well as for the shop and the charity as a whole.

The wheelchair-user who prompted the whole thing returned to the shop and cut the ribbon for the photos, just as a bit of fun. She was very happy with what we had done.

I was really satisfied that I had identified a way to make things better and had run such an innovative project so well from start to finish despite the challenges and I was really proud that I had managed to do it with zero cost to the charity. It benefitted the charity, the customers and the tradespeople, so it was very worthwhile.

The above example of an Outcomes section goes way beyond the *"It all went according to plan, and we achieved what we set out to do"* answer by detailing all of the immediate local consequences and also mentions some positive publicity for the organisation. In addition to this it touches upon the personal motivations mentioned in the Background section.

This section is your chance to show that you can see the bigger picture and you're eager to maximise the benefits of your experience by sharing anything you learned with your team, the wider organisation or with the other individuals or agencies you worked with. Sharing information is particularly relevant if it impacts on people's safety.

Someone working on a building site once told me during an interview that they modified a piece of equipment to stop people from being injured. It would have been a thousand times more impressive if he'd gone on to say he'd shared this work with the rest of the construction industry and saved thousands of injuries, or even is he'd just shared it with the rest of the building site, but he didn't bother. He kept it to himself. In the Fire Service, information like this needs to be shared.

You need to show what you learned, how you maximised the benefits, who you shared the information with and what you did/will do next.

So, to finish off our example using the BACON method, your "Now What?" section might be something like this:

Once the work was completed, I reflected on how many people had benefitted – the shop, the charity, customers, local businesses and me in terms of project management experience.

I thought about how I could use this experience to benefit as many people as possible and decided the best way of doing this would be to share it with the wider organisation.

I emailed the charity's head office describing the work and recommending it is shared amongst all their branches in the UK, encouraging managers to do similar things in their own shops. I offered to act as a point of contact for information and advice, so anyone else following my example would have someone to refer to if they had problems or queries.

I know at least six other shops locally have since worked with local businesses to complete renovation or decoration for free, as a direct result of my work.

I also contacted the Charities Commission to see if the work can be shared with the whole sector, to achieve UK-wide benefits although I'm still waiting to hear back from them.

The ultimate consequence of all this is that countless small businesses will benefit as well as all the causes which the charities exist to support, all in a way that achieves great publicity, and more inclusive facilities.

So, you can now see, from the example we've used how it is possible to use what may seem like a plain and unimpressive piece of work to demonstrate that you have all the qualities the interviewer is looking for to make sure you're suitable firefighter material.

In this example the candidate has shown that they have a commitment to diversity and integrity, an ability to work with others, effective communication, openness to change and an ability to solve problems. The example shows that they're proactive and resilient, they can think outside the box, they have keen attention to detail, consider others, can work on their own initiative, they're eager to solve problems to help others and can see the benefit of sharing information, all because they got a builder to put up a partition wall in a shop!

It's important to realise that you don't necessarily need exceptionally good evidence or experience. The most important thing is how you deliver it.

Mediocre tasks explained properly and linked to the PQAs/Quadrants score far higher than stories of fantastic deeds told poorly with no regard for the PQAs/Quadrants.

Using this format, you can show the interviewer that you think and act in the Fire Service way. You can pass the interview with evidence as humble as asking a builder to knock-up a couple of stud-walls in a shop!

You may be panicking about the size of the example we've used, and the amount of detail included in it. You may be thinking there's no way you will ever remember that amount of information. Rest easy – you will be very surprised about how much you can remember if you follow the guidance in the following sections which takes you through the final stages of interview preparation.

Also, you don't have to remember every single word! If you remember just 75% of a brilliantly written B.A.C.O.N. example, that's still way more impressive to an interviewer than someone struggling to explain the first vaguely relevant piece of work they can think about.

At this point it's worth looking at some real-world examples which show the importance of good delivery.

The Best Answer I've Ever Heard for an *"Equality and Diversity"* question.

Recently we've been asking the following question during interviews:

"What do you understand by 'diversity', and why is it important in the workplace?"

The majority of candidates probably have a reasonable idea of what diversity means but they just can't seem to define it very well. Usually, they'll say something about race or gender, then they pretty much run out of steam and find it very hard to explain why diversity is important in the workplace. However, one candidate really stood out and got top marks.

Firstly, she listed the **nine characteristics** (see Equality and Diversity section) and explained how discrimination based on these characteristics is unlawful, referencing the relevant legislation. Next, she pointed out that a workplace that values differences and encourages people to be themselves will attract people from all backgrounds, leading to a workforce with broader spread of experience, perspectives and ideas.

So far so brilliant, but what she did next took her answer to the next level. She *crowbarred-in* a really good, highly relevant example of her own experience that she had probably prepared as an answer for a *"Tell me about a time when you encountered diversity issues in the workplace"* question.

Even though the question wasn't the format she was expecting, she managed to seamlessly introduce her evidence just by saying *"I can tell you exactly why diversity is important in the workplace using a recent piece of work I was involved with..."*

The evidence was this: She worked in a large office which was part of a government department which regularly received email queries from small businesses. They had a policy of always responding within seven days to queries submitted in English, but they were allowed to take much longer to respond to foreign language emails due to the additional time needed to get them translated. In fact, there was no set timescale to respond for foreign language emails and they often took several weeks to respond.

She said that this struck her as unfair, and it really bothered her that it was disadvantaging businesspeople whose first language was not English. She immediately set about obtaining quotes from translation agencies but found it would be very expensive, and for many languages, still may not even hit the seven-day target.

But then she realised that her organisation was blessed with a great degree of diversity, and that this talent-pool was a vast, unused resource which could not only solve the problem but also demonstrate to employees how diversity can benefit the workforce. She sent out a global email to everyone in the organisation and posted an advert on their intranet homepage, asking people to register as in-house translators. Over a period of months, she established a database of volunteers who were fluent in the most commonly spoken languages in the UK.

She explained to me exactly how the system worked, with emails being farmed-out to the appropriate employees for translation. Once the system was fully operational, she said that every incoming email query was being dealt with within seven days, regardless of the language, and that this was being done at no extra cost to the organisation, as existing employees were completing the work, mainly using their own first languages.

This project was then used by the organisation as a good news story, to show employees how a diverse workforce can have real-world practical benefits.

She then looped-back to the original question, tying it all up in a neat circle, by saying *"So the second part of your question was about why diversity in the workplace is important – hopefully you can see from that example that it's not only about representing the wider population; in fact, diversity offers benefits in its own right. It's a great, positive thing, not just an obligation"*.

She scored top marks for this question. The next candidate to walk into the interview room just mumbled something about once having a female boss and that he was prepared to accept orders from women. The first candidate was a tough act to follow!

Poor Evidence Delivered Well v Good Evidence Delivered Poorly

I have actively been involved in a firefighter recruitment process during the time that I have been reviewing this chapter.

I interviewed two particular candidates, one immediately after the other and their performance may serve as a useful example of the importance of effective delivery.

Both candidates had recently left the army. They came from similar backgrounds; they were both male, both in their thirties and coincidentally both had served time in Afghanistan.

What differed most about them was the way they delivered their evidence. I will describe it here so you can see that ***the way you describe what you did is more important than what you actually did.*** I really can't emphasise this enough.

Candidate A – Great Evidence, Poor Delivery

This chap used what sounded like a very impressive experience in which he gave emergency medical treatment to a seriously injured enemy soldier in a field hospital whilst his distressed (and armed) relatives looked-on, with shells exploding within earshot.

This sounded like an incredibly high-pressure environment and must have required real self-control, guts and calmness under pressure. These are all desirable qualities for a firefighter. The fact that he was able to provide the same level of care to an enemy soldier that he provided to his own comrades *suggested* he was focused, impartial and professional. However, he didn't explore this. He sold himself short.

Also, his answer was full of statements like *"I was instructed to... my Lieutenant told me to... we had to... we ended up... I had to follow the procedure..."* He didn't sound at all dynamic or proactive; not once did he show any sign that he was capable of improvising or thinking for himself.

He came across as someone who was brilliant at following instructions but would need constant supervision at an incident in case anything unexpected happened.

Also, he didn't seem able to reflect afterwards on what went well/not so well. He was entirely focused on the immediate task in front of him and showed no inclination to improve the way things were done or share his learning experiences.

The biggest shame of all was that he appeared to have no idea of how his actions were influencing the wider organisation. In reality, all his hard work and bravery was probably winning hearts and minds on the battlefield, improving the safety of our servicemen and women and ultimately, possibly even increasing the safety of everyone in the UK by some small degree, indirectly. He just couldn't see this though and focused entirely on medical details and operational procedures.

He seemed to think that, because his story involved him being a hero, and because it sounded dramatic, then that would be enough to pass the interview, but it lacked the substance required.

I felt genuinely disappointed for him that he wasn't putting himself over better – I had a sneaking feeling he was more capable than he appeared in the interview, but despite many leading questions from me, he just didn't hit the PQAs being tested on that question (Commitment to Excellence and Openness to Change). No matter how generous I tried to be with the marking, he still failed to reach the score required. I hope he finds this book and tries again.

Candidate B – Mediocre Evidence, Great Delivery

This guy's role in Afghanistan seemed much less exciting, and also much less dangerous. He was a Quartermaster responsible for the housekeeping of a hangar full of armoured vehicles and equipment. He told a story of how he got his team to reorganise and sweep the hangar. When he started with this example, I thought it sounded very simplistic and mundane. I expected him to get quite a low score.

However, within seconds of starting his boring example, he mentioned that *nobody else has asked him to do* it and the reason he *proactively took responsibility for changing* the way the hangar was maintained was because *he had high personal standards,* and he had realised that the organisation's performance depends on all members paying attention to the details. My ears pricked up.

This guy instantly sounded like firefighter material, and he had ticked several of the boxes on the marking sheet in just a few words. He had voluntarily initiated a positive change because he could see the bigger picture and the benefits of change upon the wider organisation. Tick, tick, tick.

He went on to explain how he had managed to win-over his team members who were initially disinterested and reluctant to change the process and take on extra work, by describing to them the consequences of dirt, litter and disorder in their environment.

He managed to instil pride in his team and make them appreciate that they were vital components in a big machine. He linked high standards in the hangar to safety and efficiency of the whole operation and gave his team an appreciation of how even small tasks relate to the bigger objectives.

He explained that it is harder to ask squaddies to adhere to high standards if you are expecting them to work in a scruffy and neglected environment; hard to expect them to do a job when you can't find the kit they need, or the kit is dirty or damaged. Standards need to be consistent, and details matter – just because a job is menial it doesn't mean it doesn't have knock-on effects.

He talked about the consequences of him identifying and driving forward this work, which included an increased efficiency and less frustration when trying to find an item in the hangar, leading to equipment reaching the frontline sooner, thus improving safety and morale. He measured the improvement using a decrease in "Missing Kit Reports", and even mentioned some challenges involving his senior officer not understanding the changes and used this as learning point, saying he would make more of an effort to explain the changes to people at the start next time.

The question was designed to look at how likely a person is to make changes in order to improve things, on their own initiative. The man who saved lives on the battlefield lost out to the bloke responsible for tidying a shed, because of the way they delivered their evidence. It just goes to show how it is possible to make a very ordinary sounding piece of work hit many different criteria, and how you can't rely on exciting or glamorous stories to carry you through.

This example also shows how selecting the right example is key. You need to think hard about which PQAs are being examined by each question and pull out the most relevant answer.

We've touched on the subject of mistakes already in the "Challenges" section of B.A.C.O.N. The most impressive candidates I have interviewed have given answers involving a time when they made a significant mistake during a task. In the best examples of this, the candidate:

- Identified the mistake themselves (showing that they monitor their own work/performance)
- Owned-up to the mistake (showing that they have a high degree of honesty and integrity)
- Took steps to minimise its impact (showing that they are committed to problem solving and working to a high standard)
- Reflected on why/how they made the mistake in the first place (showing a desire to address own performance issues/learn from mistakes)
- Identified ways to prevent the problem happening again (showing their ability to think beyond the immediate task and avert future difficulties)
- Shared information with colleagues (showing good teamwork and communication skills, and desire for continuous improvement)

The very fact that they are happy to discuss their mistakes in an interview speaks volumes about their openness, maturity and professionalism.

An example of this is someone who worked for a builder; he didn't provide instructions to an apprentice who then ended up installing the wrong kind of lintel. He spotted the mistake during a routine inspection, let the homeowner know, apologised, assured them that the mistake would be corrected at no extra expense, arranged for the proper lintel to be fitted and requested additional staff from another site to ensure the extra work didn't cause any delays.

Most impressively though, he did some analysis of how the problem happened, and rather than blaming the apprentice, he realised that he himself was at fault for not providing enough guidance because he was too busy. He used this to justify an extra labourer on site; this freed-up enough time for him to oversee and mentor the apprentice properly. The result was that the work was completed to a high standard, the apprentice learned the job more effectively and his work was better and safer.

The applicant even recommended to senior management that the staffing levels on other sites / future jobs were increased during a particular phase. Management initially dismissed the idea, but he was able to justify the extra expense by pointing out that it would reduce future mistakes and the need for costly remedial work so could save money in the long run.

Look how this example hits every one of the bullet-points above. Most of my follow-up questions, such as "Were there any challenges" and "What did you learn?" were not even needed as he had already answered them.

It's Time to Get Writing

Ok, so you've completed The Matrix to identify which pieces of your life experience best illustrate the criteria being tested. Hopefully you should have whittled it down to your strongest four or five pieces of evidence. If you have any gaping holes – PQAs or NFCC Quadrants which you can't hit – then you need to have a serious think about ways of obtaining the relevant experience within the time you have available. Volunteering for something like charity work or leading on a project inside or outside of work are probably your best bets. Think carefully before you embark on anything time-consuming, to make sure it will provide you with the evidence you are currently lacking – you don't want to be wasting any time here.

Even if you do have some deficiencies, that shouldn't stop you from starting to write up the evidence you do actually have. You know all about The B.A.C.O.N. method and you've seen a solid example of how to use it, so you should be capable of writing your evidence down in the best possible way. It's time to get writing.

TASK 14

Over the next five or six pages of your notebook, write a first draft of each of your final pieces of evidence using **B.A.C.O.N.** These are the pieces of evidence you identified as your best using the Matrix table.

Title each page with the name of the evidence (e.g. *"Organising Surf Rescue Club Competition"*) and the PQA or NFCC Quadrant (depending on which criteria your Fire Service is using) that it relates to.

These first drafts do not need to be complete sentences, and they only need to make sense to you at this point, so you don't need lengthy explanations. Keep the PQAs/Quadrants themselves handy whilst you're writing, so you know what you're aiming for. It's ok to use key phrases from the PQAs/Quadrants themselves, just do so sparingly; interviewers have been known to play PQA/Quadrant Bingo.

Try to keep each piece of evidence to one page and use the subheadings *Background, Actions, Challenges, Outcomes, Now What?*

Once you've completed them, re-read them to make sure you haven't left anything out. Then re-read the PQAs/Quadrants to make sure you've hit the key points.

This is a time-consuming task. It may take you several sessions to complete. It is worth the effort though, as you are laying the foundations for some rock-solid interview answers here.

Part 7 – Rehearsals and Timing

Perfecting Your Answers

Once you have completed Task 14 you should have draft versions of five or six pieces of evidence and you should know how long you are going to have to answer to each question; most likely five minutes, maybe ten.

The next step is to perfect your evidence. We want each example to be memorable, coherent and to provide your interviewer with everything they are looking for within the time allotted.

In the next task you will hone your answers to perfection by reading them aloud, listening to how they sound, and timing yourself to ensure they are all exactly the right length.

Each time you finish reading your answer aloud, it should be clear where you need to explain something in more detail, where you are repeating something unnecessarily, where something contradicts, where you have left some important detail out or where something needs to be emphasised more to get a point across.

Your answers will get progressively better as you expand and adapt them. You will most likely end up with each answer written out several times, each one better than the previous one, and covered in scrawled amendments and additions.

It is important to keep a copy of the PQAs/Quadrants handy whilst you go through this process to keep you focused. You may find the 'charity shop' example to be a useful template when formulating your answers.

After going through several drafts involving numerous amendments, you should eventually arrive at a final version that hits all the key points and flows well.

TASK 15

Get a stopwatch or use your phone's timer. Start the clock and read each example from your notebook, talking at a normal speed.

As you do it, listen to the sound of your voice and try to imagine what it sounds like to someone who has never heard it before. Does it make sense? Is there enough background information? Have you included all the key parts? Have you explained any acronyms or jargon?

Pay attention to your tone of voice as well as your speed – try and avoid monotone and maintain a steady pace. Keep an eye on the time as you are talking to keep you on-track so you get an idea of how long each part of your answer should take and what that time feels like.

As soon as you have finished reading it out, stop the clock. Did you manage to fill the time with all the information you need to get across, delivered at a reasonable speed? If you found yourself rushing and struggling to cram it all in, you need to edit your answer down to trim off some excess. If you found you had loads of time to spare, go back over the guidance in this book and make sure you've hit all the elements of the PQAs/Quadrants being answered and achieved all the objectives laid out in the B.A.C.O.N. method.

Have you mentioned any mistakes you made, what you learned etc.?

After this first read-through, re-write your answer neatly on a new page. Include any improvements and changes that you identified.

Repeat until you are happy that your answer hits the PQAs/Quadrants and is a suitable for a likely question such as *"Tell us about a time you worked in a team"* or *"Tell us about a time you had to work in a high-pressure situation"*.

You will need to repeat Task 15 a few times for each piece of evidence, moulding it bit by bit into the finished article. By doing it this way you become increasingly familiar with the material and the speed of delivery – you're simultaneously perfecting your answers and rehearsing your delivery.

Eventually, you will be able to summarise each piece of evidence with bullet points – simple prompts that you can refer to, to keep you on-track.

TASK 16

Summarise each one of your pieces of evidence, in as few words as possible.

You may prefer to do this task on A6 record cards (also known as "prompt cards", the kind that people use when giving speeches) rather than in your book. They're about £2 a pack in any stationery shop or available online.

Use bullet-point prompts. You just need one or two words to remind you what comes next so you can just glance down at your notes if you get stuck as you're rehearsing. Just a quick abbreviated phrase to remind you what comes next if you get stuck. Something like this would do it for the Charity Shop example:

- Volunteer – motivations
- Saw poss improvement
- DDA / EA / pers reasons
- Cost-neutral
- Several ideas
- Social media
- Newspaper
- Wrong measurements...

    etc.

Finally, after rehearsing each answer several times, you should be able to recite the whole thing without referring to any notes at all.

Some people I know have recorded themselves reciting their final pieces of evidence on their phones, and they listen to them whilst driving to/from work or doing the chores, just to make sure they're 100% bang-on.

For my most recent promotion process, by the time the interview came I could recite all my evidence without even thinking about it. I had rehearsed it so many times I knew it back to front and inside-out.

Knowing Which Answer to Select

Ok, so now you have your final, perfect answers and handy summaries in bullet-point prompt format. Between them, they can hit every one of the PQAs/Quadrants being tested and in the time available. All of the hard thinking and preparation is done, and you've taken a whole lot of pressure off your future self in the interview room.

What could possibly go wrong now? Well, you could get confused and mix up your answers, which would be a shame. If you give your 'Working with Others' answer to a question about 'Development', for instance, you wouldn't do as well as if you'd selected the answer that you had spent all this time tailoring to hit the 'Development' PQA. Same with the Quadrants.

Several Fire and Rescue Services have started being kind with their questions – they tell you which PQA or Quadrant is being tested by each question, so they would ask something like:

"This question looks at the Outstanding Leadership. Tell us about a time when you have worked with people whose backgrounds are different from your own."

So that's pretty straightforward – you would know exactly what to do with that now.

Don't be surprised though, if the question does not make a direct reference to a PQA or Quadrant. You need to be on the lookout for key words and phrases that tell you which ones are being tested. Again, some Fire and Rescue Services are being kind and allocating a short time during which you can read through the questions immediately before the interview. You should spend this time analysing the questions to make sure you select your most appropriate responses.

We will look at some example questions later and you will start to automatically sense which PQA/Quadrant they're probing. The key thing to remember is that each question relates to a PQA/Quadrant, and you need to establish which one it is before you even think of speaking, so you can be sure you're using the best answer. Pay attention to the wording and focus on key words like *team, improvement, change, plan, development, differences...* they're all PQA/Quadrant indicators.

KEY POINT

In the interview you really need to analyse each question and have a good think about which PQA / NFCC Quadrant is being tested.

Look for key words that align with the criteria in Tasks 10 or 11 that you've been basing your answers on. Do not use the first answer that comes to mind.

This way you will be able to select the most appropriate answer that you have tailor-made to hit the PQA / Quadrant in question.

"Strengths-Based Interviews"

Several Fire and Rescue Services, particularly in southern England, use a slightly different format to the straightforward experience-based interview, so they won't be entirely *"Tell me about a time when you did x, y & z..."* They also incorporate some elements of psychometric testing, so they will be trying to establish your motivations, aptitudes and what drives you.

The good news is, whilst the format of the questions may be a bit different (and you will need to tailor your answers accordingly - we'll get to that in a minute) the actual qualities they will be looking for will be pretty much identical to in a standard PQA / NFCC Quadrant interview, i.e. they will be after someone who can act as a role model, be relied upon to do a professional job, manage themselves, work with all areas of the community, challenge unacceptable behaviour, be understanding, adaptable, diligent, resilient, enthusiastic etc.

So, if you've been told to expect a "Strengths-Based Interview", you should still follow the tasks in the book to identify your best evidence, but when you're writing your answers you will need to ensure you include two things:

1. When talking about things you've done, as well as focusing on the tasks and actions, you'll need to ensure you include references to your motivations. *"I noticed that x was happening which <u>bothered me because I value fairness</u>.... I decided to do y because <u>I like to help people</u>.... I realised I needed to gain a new skill to complete the work which is great as <u>I love to develop myself</u>."* etc.

2. Be prepared for the interview to be more conversational than usual, with follow-up questions, possibly designed to probe your motivations. *"What made you decide to do x, y, z? Why did you decide to do that? How did you feel?"* etc. You can really get this to work in your favour if you have plenty of positive 'motivation-based' answers banked up to use. Focus on the fact that you have a natural built-in urge to be the best you can be and to help others.

Rest assured that even though the format may be a bit different, they're still looking for exactly the same thing as usual and because of this, the preparation you have done using this book will still put you head and shoulders above anyone thinking of their answers on the spot.

KEY POINT

If you have received no indication of whether your Fire and Rescue Service is using the PQAs or the NFCC Framework as the basis for their Strengths-Based Interviews, it is advisable to use the newer system, the NFCC Framework Quadrants, mainly because they are easier for you to use.

If you have already immersed yourself in PQA-world, perhaps because you have had an interview previously, then you may wish to continue using the PQAs and that is absolutely fine if it suits you, just remember to include some evidence that you look after your mental health, as this is something new to the NFCC system, not specifically mentioned in the PQAs.

Strengths-Based Interview preparation requires you to pay particular attention to your personal motivations.

Your knowledge of the Core Code of Ethics and how you align with these values will also be useful in this kind of interview.

Surprise Question Formats

Sometimes we will throw in a question that is not in the usual *"Describe a time when you..."* format, just to vary things a bit. In a recent interview process I was involved with, one of the questions was *"Why do you think teamwork is important in the Fire and Rescue Service?"*

I could tell this question caught a few of the more well-prepared people off-guard as they had rehearsed for *"Tell us about a time you worked as part of a team"*, so suddenly their example didn't seem to fit the question.

One of the examples discussed previously (the one involving the translation of non-English emails) shows how best to deal with this. That candidate *crowbarred* her example in and made it fit the question – I could tell she had spent a lot of time perfecting the answer and she wasn't prepared to see that time wasted! This may not *sound* like the best way to deal with a surprise question format, but it is actually the best way. You're not just answering the question with an opinion, you're actually providing solid evidence to back up what you say with genuine experience and action.

So, in answer to the teamwork question above, just adapt your existing *teamwork* answer slightly, and put it in context by starting your answer with something like *"Teamwork is really important in the Fire and Rescue Service as every job you attend is a team effort and the safe and successful outcome of incidents depends on every member of the team working well with every other member. Firefighters' safety is of paramount importance, and you need to be able to rely on each other to work safely in dangerous environments. I have first-hand experience of the importance of teamwork from my experience coaching my local netball team..."* and then wheel in your pre-prepared answer, ticking every one of the boxes on my *'Working with Others'* marking sheet and getting a great mark. Bring it back around to the Fire and Rescue Service at the end by explaining how your netball/whatever experience would make you a great firefighter as you had teamwork ingrained in the way you operate.

So don't panic if the format is not quite what you expected. Your evidence is still good, and even if you have to crowbar it in like in the above example, it's likely that this is a better option than making something up on the spot. It is very unlikely that you will tick all the boxes with something you come up with off the top of your head in the interview room.

Part 8 – Test Yourself

Some Fire and Rescue Services actually include sample practice questions in the information packs they send out. I have noticed that these questions sometimes get re-used in the actual interviews themselves – almost as if the people running the interview process couldn't be bothered thinking of new questions! Be sure to go through the information pack thoroughly.

There are also practice questions available online – a quick Google search will help you here. There are some very good UK Fire Service forums which you may find useful too.

Another useful resource is the freely available *"National Firefighter Interview Practice Booklet"* produced by the Department for Communities and Local Government (even though this was produced way back in 2006 it is still relevant to PQA-based interviews). You can access a copy at www.is.gd/ffpractice

The NFCC has assembled a bank of questions used by UK Fire and Rescue Services. I recommend you have a look as it is excellent material for testing yourself. You can access it here: **www.is.gd/nfccquestions**

Now you have a ready-to-use set of answers, it's time to put yourself to the test. The next exercise will give you some experience in interpreting questions to establish the PQA being examined; it will also test your ability to select and recall the appropriate answer.

TASK 17

Put your notebook to one side.

Pick a random question from the following list of sample questions (or he NFCC question bank mentioned above) and answer it using one of your prepared answers.

Start the clock as soon as you begin your answer and keep an eye on it. Stick to the time limit.

You may have an answer that fits the question perfectly, thanks to the work you have done. Just remember to *actually answer the question*, as obvious as that may sound – don't concentrate entirely on hitting the PQAs/Quadrants.

You may need to briefly improvise to address any specifics of the question if it's not already covered by your prepared answer.

When you have asked yourself one of these questions, tick it off.

Over a period of days, you should be able to answer all of these example questions. This will hone your skills, enabling you to smell the testing criteria a mile off and shoot it down easily.

This task can go on for as long as you like, and the more questions you test yourself on, the better and more adaptable you will become.

If you have a friend, partner or family member who is willing to help out, once you become more confident it's actually better to have someone else firing the questions at you. This way will get used to making eye contact as you speak – it's quite different to blabbering on with nobody listening.

Don't get people to ask you the questions until you're good and ready though as it could undermine your confidence if you make a hash of it in front of a witness.

Common Interview Questions

Here are some of the questions most commonly used in UK Fire and Rescue Service firefighter recruitment interviews, with some pointers to help you segue into your prepared answers.

Tell us about a time you have worked as part of a team and had to motivate people to get work done.

You should expect a *"Team"* question. Look out for any extra twists though. With this one, people tended to focus solely on the *team* bit, and they missed the crucial *motivation* aspect. Be sure to answer the question fully.

What is your understanding of the role of Firefighter?

You did a whole section on this subject, involving a lot of preparation, so you should absolutely *nail* this question.

One of Westhampton Fire and Rescue Service's core values is Discipline. Tell me why you think discipline is so important in the Fire and Rescue Service.

You should cover self-discipline, respect, and adherence to procedures. Discuss benefits of good discipline to self, team, organisation and community.

We work to reduce risk in all areas of the community. Which areas do you think we should be focusing on in your community and why? What messages should we be trying to get across and how?

You can impress your interviewer here with your knowledge of what your Fire Service is currently engaged in, in terms of risk reduction. Focus on one element that is particularly relevant in your area; or if there's nothing happening locally, anything more general involving our ageing population is a safe bet.

You may be asked a follow-up question about which other groups need targeting; choose a totally different area, for instance if you speak first about home safety / safe-and-well visits for the elderly, move on to talking about targeting teenage drivers with RTC reduction work. By covering two different areas of FRS work you will demonstrate you've done your research. It also shows that you appreciate the need for a firefighter to be able to adapt their communication methods and content in order to reach all groups within the community.

Note: We have recently been asking *"What are the challenges facing the Fire and Rescue Service?"* – a similar answer is needed with additional "culture review" references.

Give me an example of a time when you have built new relationships with team members.

Your *"Working with Others"* PQA / *"Outstanding Leadership"* Quadrant example should answer this one perfectly.

When was the last time you learned a new skill?

If, as recommended earlier, you have visited a Fire Station as part of your research, you may have learned new skills which are directly relevant to the role of firefighter such as hose-running. This is the ideal time to mention this as it shows your ability to focus on your own development.

It's ok to admit that you found learning the new skill difficult, just as long as you focus on the fact that you persevered, and your determination and willingness to put in the effort and maybe adapt to a new learning style got you through it.

What are your strengths and weaknesses?

This is an over-used question, and it still crops up regularly. Your Excellence question should fit, but you will be expected to own up to a weakness –the mistake/learning experience you incorporated into that answer should help you. A weakness is fine, just as long as you can show what you are doing to deal with it.

If you're really stuck for a weakness, "impatience" is a good one, surprisingly, if you talk about how you value efficiency and you really have to discipline yourself to be patient with others who are slower than you at completing tasks. Emphasise that you never let impatience get the better of you, and you appreciate the needs of others, to highlight your empathy, self-awareness and self-discipline.

This way, you're using a supposed weakness to make yourself look good – you're showing that you are aware of your own faults and are able to compensate. You are also very productive and understanding of others' differences. Not everyone can be as good as you!

"Perfectionism" is another weakness that people often use to answer this question, and whilst it's not a very original answer it still ticks the box. Candidates have stated that they find it hard to delegate tasks to colleagues when they like to take personal responsibility for ensuring things are done to a high standard and they know they could do a good job themselves. Candidates often show that they are dealing with this weakness by making a conscious effort to delegate where appropriate and by reassuring themselves that, as long as tasks are allocated to the right people with relevant skills, then this kind of work sharing helps build resilience and trust and makes the team more productive and efficient.

More Interview Questions

Tell me about a time when you have worked to resolve an issue that was negatively impacting your team.

Tell me about a time when you have acted with sensitivity to someone's feelings or wellbeing.

Give me an example of when you have completed a task or project to a high standard.

Tell me about a time when you have been unhappy with the standard of work being produced.

Give me an example of how you have worked proactively to meet objectives.

Tell me about a time when you had a difficult conversation.

Give me an example of when you have encouraged someone to improve.

Give me an example of when your colleagues or teammates have learnt from you.

Tell me about a time when you have acted with consideration of someone's needs that were different to your own, e.g. working with a different age group, ethnicity, religion etc.

Give me an example of when you have investigated the needs of someone that was different to you in cultural background, age, gender, religion, disability etc.

Give me an example of how you have taken responsibility for your own actions.

Tell me about a time when you have been trusted with a task or information that was sensitive.

Give me an example of how you have promoted the values of a group or organisation that you belonged to.

TASK 18 (Optional)

You may feel that the above example questions and the ones compiled by the NFCC are sufficient and that you have practiced enough.

If you need more though, Google *"UK Fire Service sample interview questions"* and set yourself the task of answering some more.

Each time you answer a question, focus on:

1. Picking out the PQA/NFCC Quadrant being examined;
2. Selecting your most relevant pre-prepared answer;
3. Remembering and reciting your answer well; and
4. Ensuring you have actually answered the question.

This last point is very important and sometimes easy to forget if you're obsessing over PQAs/NFCC Quadrants.

PART 8 - SUMMARY

Once you have answered a load of practice questions, it becomes second-nature to hear a question and know which PQA/NFCC Quadrant is being tested. Remembering which one of your answers fits each criterion also comes naturally with practice. The more you practice, the easier the interview will be. The sample questions above should be enough, but if you need more, internet forums are a good place to look.

It's common sense really. Are they asking about teamwork? Ok, it's Working with Others/Outstanding Leadership. Are they asking about changing / improving? Right – that's Excellence/Organisational Effectiveness, and so on. You've got this.

Wherever possible and appropriate, drop in references to local risks and initiatives so you can show that you are switched-on about your area and your Fire Service.

Part 9 – Interview Tips & Etiquette

Some simple tips now to make sure you're in the right mind-set on the day and you create a great impression.

Visualisation

I used to think that this kind of thing was mumbo-jumbo nonsense until I read a book called *Trick of the Mind* by the renowned mentalist Derren Brown. I have used it though, and I know it really works, I promise you.

Basically, if you keep envisaging the worst things that can happen – picturing yourself clamming-up in the interview, embarrassing yourself, stuttering, blushing and forgetting your lines, then these things are actually more likely to happen. By imagining these things, you are effectively *rehearsing for them to happen.* It's like training yourself to fail. You are reinforcing the neural pathways in your brain that relate to exactly the behaviour you want to avoid, so your fears become self-fulfilling.

What you need to do instead picture all those things disappearing down a hole, and try not to think of any negative possibilities again.

Instead, envisage yourself performing at your very best. You need to reinforce the pathways in your brain that relate to good performance and positive experience.

Picture yourself talking confidently in the interview, with the interviewers watching you, nodding, interested in what you are saying. You are in full-flow, enthusiastic and confident; everything is going as planned and you can tell they like you.

Picture yourself walking out of the interview, having totally nailed it. Imagine the feeling inside – that barely containable sense of joy and satisfaction that you've done your very best. You punch the air in celebration. What a feeling!

Imagine how you'll feel on the journey home after your successful interview. You will be filled with a sense of satisfaction. When people ask how you did in your interview, you'll feel warm inside and you will even have to tone-down your answer as you don't want to look cocky and overconfident, but inside you'll know you *nailed it.*

Whenever you find yourself worrying about the upcoming interview, use it as a cue to employ this technique. That way, instead of getting stressed about it, you will be doing something incredibly positive and productive instead – a mental rehearsal of success. You may think this sounds like psychobabble like I did initially, but it really does work.

Your Appearance

People judge you on your appearance, no matter how hard they try to be unbiased; it's an unavoidable human trait. You need to look the part.

Have a tidy haircut a few days before the interview. A smart new haircut can transform your appearance from scruffy and unkempt to sharp and smart. It also adds to your self-esteem and confidence. If you've got some kind of crazy funky hairstyle that you've spent years cultivating, don't worry – you're entitled to your individuality, just remember that you're applying to be a public servant, not a rock star, so bear than in mind and perhaps flatten-down the Mohawk just for the day.

You should ideally wear a suit (dark blue, black or grey) and if you identify/present yourself as male, a tie, as this projects professionalism and maturity. Obviously those who identify/present as female may also wish to wear a tie, but the lack of tie somehow matters less. A tie also shows due respect to the organisation, the process and the interviewer. Research has shown that blue ties create an impression of confidence, reliability and honesty – ideal for the Fire and Rescue Service. Red is supposed to suggest assertiveness and confidence, so maybe go for this is you are meek and nervous but avoid it if you are already a cocky character.

I have previously given jobs to people who wore polo shirts, but they had to recover from minus-points the moment they walked into the room. What's the point of giving yourself a handicap when you could be impressing the interviewer? I know for a fact that a colleague once binned an applicant's exam paper as he wore a baseball cap to the test centre. No dress-code had been provided to candidates, but the examiner decided that, by wearing a baseball cap to a recruitment event, the candidate had showed poor judgement and did not understand the importance of standards of appearance. These things happen, and people are still quite old-fashioned.

At least a week before the interview, select what you are going to wear. Actually get it out of the wardrobe and check it. This is especially important if you haven't worn it since that wedding three years ago. It might still be covered in food, mildew or worse. Give it a sniff-test and get it dry-cleaned if it's fusty. You need to make sure everything is clean and pristine, perfectly ironed, shoes clean and polished. Self-discipline and standards are very important qualities in the Fire and Rescue Service.

If you haven't got a suit, borrow or buy one. Failing that, a smart, ironed long-sleeved shirt, tie and smart trousers or skirt. It's always good to smell nice too, but remember that you only need a couple of squirts of your favourite scent to create a good impression.

An operational firefighter is expected to cover any piercings whilst on-duty, for health and safety reasons. You won't be expected to do this in the interview but if you usually wear flamboyant piercings, maybe wear something more discreet if possible.

If you have a beard, make it tidy. If not, have a shave on the morning of the interview. That in-between stage of few days' growth is unkempt and grubby looking, giving an impression of poor personal hygiene. Conversely, if it's November, pretty much any weird or ridiculously dodgy Movember-themed facial adornment is not only forgiven but can actually go in your favour as it suggests you're good-humoured and keen to help others. Just be ready to answer questions about how the fundraising is going.

Don't worry though – you don't need to look like a 1940's accountant just to be accepted in the interview. I have given jobs to some pretty whacky looking people in the past; just be mindful of the impression you create.

Logistics

Plan how you are going to get to the interview location. Your main aim is to get there *early*, feeling fresh and unflustered, so don't leave anything to chance. Make 100% sure you've got the right time, date and place. If the interview is in the morning and/or a long way away, it may be best to book a hotel nearby the night before (in which case, plan how you're getting to the venue from the hotel). If you are driving there, put the postcode into Google Maps and check the estimated travel time to give you the required departure time. Make sure your car is ok and not likely to break down on the way. Take cash in case the worst happens, and you have to get a taxi.

Make a note of the contact number on the interview invitation letter so that you can call ahead and let them know if something out of your control is going to make you late.

It may be possible for them to reschedule things if you provide enough notice and sometimes things are out of your hands. Someone called us once to say he was going to be late because someone had jumped in front of his train – we couldn't really hold that against him and the fact that he rang us straight away showed he was keen to make things work; we were able to fit him in later that day. I did double-check his story mind, and it checked-out, so don't ring up with a verifiable lie if you're just running late, in case you're caught out.

Make sure you don't have any clashes on the day of the interview. The last thing you want is a phone call from your partner asking why you haven't picked the kids up, just as you're walking into the interview. Also, don't assume the interview will be over in any set time. I once had a candidate panicking in her interview because we were overrunning, and she was going to be late for her train. You really need to block off a good few hours either side of the interview to make sure you can focus all your brainpower on it and not have anything nagging at your subconscious.

If you use Outlook or a similar electronic calendar in work, block off the whole day as soon as possible to stop anyone booking you for other events.

For my promotion interviews, they say to arrive 15 minutes before the interview, but I always drive to the venue and get there over an hour before that, so probably a full hour and a half before the interview. I park in a nearby supermarket car park and read through my notes one final time. Knowing I'm only a couple of minutes' drive from the venue keeps me nice and calm – it's like I've already cleared the first hurdle. Then, with 20 mins to go I just nip round the corner and sign in at the venue. I recommend doing something similar – even if you do have transport issues, the fact that you were aiming for 90 mins before the start time gives you a nice buffer, avoiding any panic.

If you smoke, don't smoke in the car on the way to the interview. Candidates that stink of cigarette smoke don't come across as the kind of people we want representing the Fire Service. Smoke out in the open, out of sight, if you really have to. Brush your teeth afterwards if possible, or use gum/toothpaste and a small amount of aftershave. Some interviewers are *very* anti-smoking.

Make sure you're not hungry or thirsty during the interview. I always have a decent breakfast on a big day and then a banana and a coffee shortly before an interview or presentation, to make sure I'm fuelled-up and alert.

Arrival

Before you even arrive at venue, assume everyone is your interviewer. That bloke that just pulled-out in front of you? You may regret beeping and swearing at him in an hour's time when he's sat on the other side of the desk. This has happened.

Turn your mobile phone to silent. Flight mode is better, leaving it in the car is better still. You don't need any distractions, and a mid-interview novelty ringtone is embarrassing, unprofessional and will disrupt your flow.

When you get into the venue, assume you are being watched in the car park. No smoking, littering, spitting gum etc. Walk tall; be confident. The best way to walk tall without strutting is to pretend there's a thread pulling you up from the top of your head – it works. Greet anyone you see with a friendly smile.

Report to reception. They will be expecting you and you will probably have to sign in and get a temporary ID badge. Be very polite to the receptionist. I've had a receptionist complain that a candidate was rude to her – he didn't get the job.

Now is probably a good time for a quick visit to the toilet, for a few reasons, the obvious one being that you don't want to be desperate for a pee during the interview. Also, it's a good time for a final check of your appearance. Make sure your hair is in place, there's nothing stuck in your teeth and your tie is straight. Take your time, wash your hands; breathe deeply; stay calm. You've got this. Also, if you notice that you're dehydrated, you need to get a drink ASAP as your brain won't be functioning at 100% unless you get some water on-board.

If you've been using the visualisation technique mentioned previously, now is probably your last opportunity to picture yourself emerging victorious from the interview room!

Right, You're Up!

Eventually, someone will come and get you from reception. Whoever that person is, smile when they greet you and be polite and courteous. If they engage you in casual chit-chat, they are probably trying to make you calm and comfortable. They are being professional, so make sure your small talk is appropriate.

Whether you get put in a holding-room to read the questions, or you are taken straight into the interview room, you will eventually meet your interviewer/s. If you are sat down when you meet them, stand up and shake their hands firmly but don't crush them. It's a classic rule of etiquette not to shake hands sat down. If they haven't already said your name, then you should introduce yourself – they know who you are, but it is polite.

The Interview Itself

The whole of this book is aimed at making sure you know exactly what to *say* in a Fire and Rescue Service interview. The way to *act* in a Fire Service interview though, is not much different from how you would act in any other interview, and there is a wealth of information online providing guidance on interview etiquette. For this reason, I have only summarised the most important areas here, just to make sure you avoid the worst mistakes. I recommend searching YouTube for *"Interview Etiquette"* for further advice in this area.

Be smart, courteous and on-time – see above.

Don't swear. At all. Ever. Not once. Even if a swear-word forms part of a story you are telling, do not say the word itself. This is *very* important and there are no exceptions.

Swearing in interviews is not acceptable, ever. Even fairly inoffensive words like *"crap"* are not appropriate in an interview. They just hang in the air like embarrassing mistakes.

Don't interrupt the interviewer – that's very bad form and shows a lack of respect. If you do it accidentally, apologise and allow the interviewer to finish.

If you are provided with pen and paper, write down your format to keep you from straying off course. Whether you're using S.T.A.R. or B.A.C.O.N. you will benefit from having it there in black and white. If you have time alone with the questions, write down the names of the examples you are going to use, and the key points of each one. NOTE: You will probably have to hand in all paperwork at the end, so don't write (or draw) anything you don't want the interviewer to see.

Listen very closely to the questions. If a printed version of the questions is provided, read it carefully and underline the key words if they're not already highlighted. If no printed version is provided, write down the key words of each question as it is being asked.

Ask the interviewer to repeat the question if you are in any doubt. If you find yourself halfway through your answer and it feels like you've lost track or gone off on a tangent, it's ok to ask for the question to be repeated again at this point. Say something like *"Please can you repeat the question, just to make sure I'm answering it fully?"* so you don't sound too scatter-brained/forgetful.

Pause... before answering. This is a powerful technique, and it helps you to take control of the pace. Take a couple of seconds to compose yourself, focus, and take a deep breath. After all you've done to prepare, it's crucial that you don't just launch into the first thing that comes into your head. This is especially important if your interviewer is a fast talker as the temptation is to carry on at the pace they finished at. A nice pause makes it easier to start at your own pace.

It's actually funny sometimes when you do this. The interviewer reaches the end of the question and it's over to you, then... silence. You will often find that the interviewer shifts uncomfortably in their seat at this point as it feels a little awkward, but that's ok. It's just you regaining a little control and beginning to own the room. Five to ten seconds of silence is ideal.

Don't rush. Nerves mean you will find yourself speeding up, and you need to hold yourself back. Talking at a normal pace gives the impression of confidence, and also gives you more time to think of what to say next and stay on-track. You need to avoid your mouth going faster than your brain. You've rehearsed the timings, and you know you can say everything required in the time given so there is no need to rush it. Take it steady.

Don't fidget. Try and find a position that you're comfortable with but don't slouch. Mirroring the position of your interviewer is often a good technique. The look you're aiming for is "attentive and enthusiastic". Crossed arms are seen as defensive body language. Loosely clasped hands resting on the table or your lap looks good but feel free to use your hands whilst talking if that's your habit.

Don't try and be funny. You may be nervous, but trying to break the ice with comedy will backfire and you will end up looking like an unprofessional joker.

Avoid slang, explain acronyms and jargon. When talking about something technical, imagine you are talking to a very intelligent 16-year-old – in other words, someone who doesn't have much life experience so needs everything explaining, but once you explain it properly, they are quite capable of understanding anything.

As we talked about in the Equality and Diversity section, avoid male-specific words like fireman (firefighter), policeman (police officer), manned (staffed or crewed) etc.

Be enthusiastic. You really want this job, so show it, but beware of seeming desperate.

Your interviewer may ask *"Is there anything else you would like to add?"* every time you finish answering. Don't be unnerved by this – they're not prompting you to mention something obvious that you left out, it's just a standard follow-up question, usually used when there is a bit of time left on the clock. So, it might mean you are going too fast; use it as a prompt to stop, reflect over the answer you have just given, think if you missed anything important, take a breath, and move on at a nice steady pace.

You will probably be asked if you have any questions of your own at the end. Don't ask anything dopey or something that you should know anyway, like what's the salary of a firefighter (just Google it).

You may want to ask when the results are likely to come out, or how long successful candidates will remain on the waiting list for (sometimes candidates get put in a pool and have to wait for a job to come up).

I have a personal favourite question to ask whenever I'm being interviewed for a job. It's one that I have used numerous times as a kind of safeguard or a last resort to clear up any potential misunderstanding.

It puts interviewers on the spot a bit, which is why I love asking it:

"Have I said anything, of left anything out that has given you any concerns or reservations? Anything that would affect my chances of getting the job? I would really hate to miss out on the basis of a misunderstanding so I would be happy to clear up any issues now."

If an otherwise great candidate ever asked me this question, I think I would happily revisit any niggling doubts I had if they'd said something which gave me doubts about their suitability, just to give them a final chance to explain.

TASK 19

Your final task, and it's a simple one. Make yourself a checklist of everything you need to consider or arrange to make sure you arrive at the interview on time, looking your best and feeling fresh, focused, and positive. We've been through pretty much every possible consideration in this section, but you may have other needs specific to you – medication, contact lenses, your nan's cat, whatever. Don't leave anything to chance.

Use Google Maps to plan your journey to the interview location as it gives you the ability to select a desired arrival time, which factors in usual traffic conditions at that time of day. Aim to get there, or to a nearby car park where you can wait safe in the knowledge that you're not going to be late, *at least* half an hour before the time you've been told to arrive. Use this time to compose yourself, check your notes one last time, and visualise success.

Good Luck?

I am a firm believer in the idea that you make your own luck. The world's most successful people frequently say they got lucky and that they were in the right place at the right time. In reality what happened is that they *put themselves* in the right place, and they were *prepared to act* when the right time came. It's this tendency to "make your own luck" that marks out successful people.

It happened to me. A colleague had to apply around a dozen times to different brigades before he finally got a job. He recently asked me how many attempts it took me to get into the Fire Service. *"I got in first time – I suppose I was lucky!"* was my reply. On reflection though, I made my own luck. I left nothing to chance; I did a huge amount of research and preparation and made absolutely sure that I blew the interviewer away when my time came. Nothing was going to stop me, and nothing was left to chance.

If you have followed all the steps in this book, then you have done pretty much everything you can to smash the interview. You have made your own luck.

So rather than wish you good luck, I have the following message...

You know what to do.

Go and do it!

Any Feedback on this Book?

If you enjoyed this book, *please* leave a positive review on Amazon. Some firefighter preparation books are terrible, and I genuinely believe this is the most useful, but people won't know that without positive reviews to help them find it.

I really hope that this book has been useful to you. If you have any feedback, please let me know at the email address below. Maybe you found one of the exercises particularly useful or a certain part needed more explaining. Perhaps you would like to see something extra that hasn't been covered. I welcome any comments as they will help me make the book better in future.

Also, if you send me details of your interview, the format, the questions, etc. then I can incorporate your information into future editions – by reading this book, you yourself have benefitted from those successful candidates who have gone before you – several nuggets of information in the book came from past readers via email!

I don't maintain this book for profit. The earnings from Amazon don't even cover the time it takes me to update it each year. It's really just my attempt to help good people get into what I genuinely believe is one of the best jobs in the world. By sending me details of your interview you will be helping the firefighters of the future!

All the best in your career and stay safe.

Andy Smith – getinto999@gmail.com

You can scan this code with your phone to leave a review

Or type this link into your search box: **www.is.gd/reviewlink**

Glossary

ACRONYM / TERM	STANDS FOR / MEANS	EXPLANATION
ACFO	Assistant Chief Fire Officer	The second highest rank in most Fire and Rescue Services. One rank below CFO. Assistant Commissioner in London Fire Brigade.
ADC	Assessment and Development Centre	The place (usually Fire Service Headquarters or Training School) where the selection process takes place. Also, the process itself.
AFA	Automatic Fire Alarm	A detection and warning system designed to provide early warning of fire usually in commercial premises; also used to describe an incident originating from such a system.
BA	Breathing Apparatus	Equipment used by firefighters to facilitate safe breathing in irrespirable atmospheres.
BAME / BME	Black, Asian and Minority Ethnic / Black and Minority Ethnic	Used interchangeably to refer to members of any non-white communities in the UK
B.A.C.O.N.	Background, Action, Challenges, Outcomes, Now What?	Enhanced version of the S.T.A.R. mnemonic, designed to enable candidates to answer interview questions in a way specifically tailored to Fire Service interviews.

BARS	Behaviourally Anchored Rating Scales	A scale used to mark a candidate's performance in an interview. An interviewer has to compare your answer against four columns showing varying standards of response, each column giving you a different amount of points. Google *firefighter generic BARS* to see an example.
CBRNe	Chemical, Biological, Radiological, Nuclear and Explosive	Usually used in terms of a terrorist attack. Several Fire Services and the UK's National Resilience facilities have procedures and resources to deal with an attack by these means.
CCA	Civil Contingencies Act 2004	The piece of legislation which directs Fire Services, other emergency services, local authorities, utilities, environment, and transport agencies to work together to plan for emergencies.
CFO	Chief Fire Officer	The most senior rank in a Fire and Rescue Service / Fire Brigade. Known as Fire Master in Scotland and Commissioner in London.
CFOA	Chief Fire Officers' Union	See NFCC
CM	Crew Manager	One grade up from Firefighter, usually managed by a Watch Manager. Also used by Control Room staff.
DIM	Detection, Identification, Monitoring	The process, or the facilities, used to deal with unidentified hazardous materials.
E&D	Equality and Diversity	See Part 2.
FI	Fire Investigation	The methodical and scientific way of establishing the cause and origin of a fire.

FBU	Fire Brigades' Union	The main trade union for Fire Service staff (Ff up to CFO) and Control Room staff, with around 44,000 members.
FF or Ff	Firefighter	The entry-level grade of the UK Fire Service. Usually Probationary FF during training school, then Development FF until fully qualified as a Competent FF. Also used by Control Room staff.
FMR	Fire Medical Response	Fire Service response to medical incidents, either together with or instead of the Ambulance Service. Usually limited to a specific range of medical problems such as cardiac arrest. A contentious area – see FBU website for further information.
FRS	Fire and Rescue Service	Most *Fire Brigades* have now changed their names to *Fire and Rescue Service* (with London Fire Brigade being a notable exception) to reflect the varied duties they perform and make themselves sound less military.
FRSA	Fire & Rescue Services Association	Formerly the RFU, the Retained Firefighters' Union.
HazMat	Hazardous Material	Fire Services are frequently called upon to deal with deliberate or accidental release of dangerous substances and so have developed specialised training, resources, and procedures to respond.
HMICFRS or HMIC of HMI	His Majesty's Inspectorate Of Constabulary and Fire and Rescue Services	The independent inspector of police forces (in England and Wales), and fire and rescue services (in England only).
IPDS	Integrated Personal Development System	Framework used to identify, attract, assess, and develop people to fulfil their current and future roles.

JESIP	Joint Emergency Services Interoperability Principles	A national program that aims to improve the way emergency services work together during major incidents.
LF	Leading Firefighter	The old name for Crew Manager, readopted by LFB in 2019. See CM.
LFB	London Fire Brigade	The UK's largest Fire and Rescue Service in terms of wholetime firefighter numbers.
MTA or MTFA	Marauding Terrorist Attack or Marauding Terrorist Firearms Attack	Terrorist attack designed to inflict large numbers of casualties, e.g. Mumbai 2008 & Nairobi 2013. Several Fire Services have developed dedicated capabilities to respond to such incidents. See FBU website for further information.
NFCC	National Fire Chiefs' Council	Previously known as CFOA. The professional body representing senior fire officers in the United Kingdom.
NR	National Resilience	Arrangements and equipment used to respond to major incidents, emergencies, and disruptive events.
PDA	Predetermined Attendance	The prearranged response to a type of incident. A certain number of appliances and officers will automatically be attached to a confirmed high-rise fire, for instance.
PQA/PQAs	Personal Qualities and Attributes	The personal traits required to gain entry into the Fire and Rescue Service. The things you will be trying to prove in the interview such as your ability to work with others, to act appropriately in conflict situations, to be part of a team and to communicate effectively. See PQAs section.
RFU	Retained Firefighters' Union	See FRSA

RRO	Regulatory Reform (Fire Safety) Order 2005	The piece of legislation which directs Fire Services to conduct Fire Safety activities in England and Wales.
RTC	Road Traffic Collision	A collision involving powered vehicle/s on a road or other public area.
SOP	Standard Operating Procedure	The set method of dealing with a specific type of incident. Each Fire Service will have a set of written SOPs covering RTCs, Aircraft Incidents, Confined Space rescues etc. You *can* deviate from the SOP as long as you can justify it.
SC	Station Commander	Rank above Station Officer and beneath Group Commander in LFB.
SM	Station Manager	Rank above Watch Manager and beneath Group Manager in most UK Fire and Rescue Services.
S.T.A.R.	Situation, Task, Action, Result	Standard mnemonic for answering interview questions.
UFS/UwFS	Unwanted Fire Signal	A fire call originating from an AFA which subsequently turned out to be a false alarm.
WM	Watch Manager	The third grade up in the UK Fire Service. Usually one per watch, with overall control of the watch and small to medium incidents.
WM(A)	Watch Manager (A)	Lower of the two-tier Watch Manager system, now known as Sub Officer in LFB.
WM(B)	Watch Manager (B)	Higher of the two-tier Watch Manager system, now known as Station Officer in LFB.
Watch	Team of personnel assigned to a particular shift on a Fire Station / Control Room.	To ensure a Fire Station or Control Room is crewed 24/7, a shift system of (usually four) watches works a shift pattern of days and nights. This pattern varies greatly between Fire Services. Generally, they are named after colours.

Blank PQA Matrix

EXAMPLE	WORKING WITH OTHERS	COMMITMENT TO DIVERSITY & INTEGRITY	COMMITMENT TO EXCELLENCE	COMMITMENT TO DEVELOPMENT	EFFECTIVE COMMUNICATION	OPENNESS TO CHANGE	PROBLEM SOLVING	CONFIDENCE AND RESILIENCE	SITUATIONAL AWARENESS	TOTALS

Blank NFCC Quadrant Matrix

EXAMPLE	PERSONAL IMPACT	OUTSTANDING LEADERSHIP	ORGANISATIONAL EFFECTIVENESS	SERVICE DELIVERY	TOTALS

Printed in Great Britain
by Amazon